LoveEd
LEVEL 1

BOYS THAT ARE STRONG, SMART AND PURE

LoveEd

LEVEL 1

BOYS ^{THAT}_{ARE} STRONG, SMART _{AND} PURE

Nihil Obstat
Reverend John Balluff, STD
Censor Deputatus
April 29, 2016

Permission to Publish
Most Reverend Joseph Siegel, DD, STL
Vicar General
Diocese of Joliet
May 2, 2016

Published in the United States by
Saint Benedict Press
PO Box 410487
Charlotte, NC 28241
www.SaintBenedictPress.com

Printed in the United States of America

Contents

LoveEd: An Introduction for Parents

It's no secret that today's culture is confused about love and sex. Movies, television, the Internet, and music expose children at an early age to twisted perceptions of romance and relationships. In a culture that is morally adrift, parents need the right tools to help them navigate their children safely through the dangerous temptations and distorted perceptions of sexuality.

As you attend the *LoveEd* event and work through the rest of this book with your child at home, both of you will discover the amazing truth that human sexuality has a wonderful meaning and purpose. That vocational purpose is passed on from generation to generation for those who love God and seek to serve Him, and is fulfilled when a man and a woman create a new family on their wedding day. In this family circle, children will learn how to love God, others, and themselves. *LoveEd* will help parents guide their children through the circles of love: *God's love, family love, friendship love, and an understanding of a future romantic love.*

Through the experience of this program, and along with their parents' help, children will learn that:

- God has made them to be a loving human person, both body and soul.
- God has planned for them to go through physical changes called puberty.
- God has called them to be strong, smart, and pure throughout their lives.
- God has created them to receive His love and share this amazing and pure love with others.

Level 1 of the *LoveEd* program will discuss the physical changes that occur during puberty and how these begin to prepare children for married life. It will also explain the male and female powers to co-create life with God. Level 2 will explain how a child is created through God's natural and supernatural plan, and how a baby grows in the mother's womb from conception to birth. The Parent Training Event and accompanying *Parent Guide* provide you with additional information to assist you in communicating these sacred messages to your child and answering other related questions that may arise over time.

However, it is not enough for children to know about bodily functions. Human beings are much more than biological cells and systems—we are persons made in God's image! Working through *LoveEd* will give you the tools you need to teach, from a Christ-centered perspective, about some of the important changes that will be going on in your children's bodies during the next few years, as well as the vital connection puberty has with their vocation to love and the development of virtues. When virtues are practiced, especially chastity, it can lead your children to a life of self-giving love and truly prepare them for adulthood.

Your children have the right and responsibility to know information about their growth, which is both biological and spiritual. God's special plan for sexuality is best discussed in a personal conversation with you in the context of sound Church teaching. Attending this event and reading this book will help you and your children start the conversations that will help them understand themselves and their place in God's plan.

LoveEd can be the beginning, or the continuation, of those ongoing conversations with your children about life, love, and purity, conversations that can extend into their adulthood. It's important, now more than ever, for you to guide them while they develop a holy awe of God's amazing creation of life!

PART I

Parent/Child Event

Complete the following six Acts by watching each video and answering the discussion questions with your Dad.

ACT 1

The Story of You

Introduction

The first Act introduces us to a fifth grade boy named Joey Sullivan, as well as his family and friends. We will see him in his daily life and watch as he handles some of the struggles that come with growing older.

 Watch Act I

Father and Son Discussion

Read these questions and answer them with your Dad.

1. How is the Sullivan family like your family?
   - ☑ They all live in the same house.
   - ☑ I have to take out the garbage like Joey.
   - ☑ Joey has an older brother.
   - ☐ There are little kids in the family.
   - ☑ They eat together at the dinner table.
   - ☐ Other similar things include: _____.

2. How is the Sullivan family different from yours?
   - ☑ Their parents are married, but mine are not.
   - ☑ I am the youngest, but Joey is not.
   - ☐ I am the oldest, but Joey is not.
   - ☑ They have a dog.
   - ☐ Other differences include: _____ .

3. What did Joey do that was good?
   - ☑ He was kind to Rob.
   - ☑ He made his little brother laugh.
   - ☑ He took out the garbage.
   - ☑ He helped his little sister color her picture.
   - ☐ He stood up to Greg.

4. Did you like Greg?
   - ☐ Yes, he was good at sports.
   - ☑ No, because he made fun of Rob.
   - ☑ No, because he ripped Michael's phone away and sent a mean text.
   - ☐ Yes, because he took charge.

5. If you were Joey, would you have picked Rob for your team? Why or why not?
   Yes, because he was
   my friend.

6. Ask your Dad to tell you a story of a time he was bullied as a kid. Was there a time he was the one doing the bullying? Ask him what he learned or regretted about those times.

When you get older you should not pick on people.

7. When Joey asked his dad what to do about Rob, Mr. Sullivan said, "Rob's a good kid. He just needs a good friend like you." Ask your Dad for advice. What would he have told you to do if you were in Joey's shoes?

Be a good friend and stick up for him.

8. When Joey told his dad how Greg treats Rob, Mr. Sullivan said, "If you want to be a man, you have to stand up for people that need protecting." Would you stick up for a friend who was being picked on like Joey did for Rob? Why or why not? If yes, how would you do it?

Yes, By telling them to stop.

In anticipation of viewing the Act 2 video, please complete the following activity.

At the center of the circle named "Family," write the names of the people in your immediate family and/or those who live in your home. On the outside edge of that circle, write the names of other close family members, such as grandparents and close cousins or relatives you see often and love very much.

At the center of the circle named "Friends," write the names of your closest or favorite friends. On the outside edge of that circle, write the names of other kids you hang around with.

In the next Act, we'll learn what the third dotted circle is and why you are not yet within it, but might be one day in the future.

Evan Deb Rob Grant Connor

Neva

Rick Gard

Mark, Nicole, Emma, Owen, Brody, Bailey

FAMILY

Alex Calben Charlie Kade Parker, Matthew Joe Ryan

FRIENDS

Logan

Affirming the Good

Ask your Dad to tell you about a time he was proud of you.
Have him write it down so you can read it later.

Brody,
I'm proud of you when
you help people, do good in
school and listen to me, Also
when you do good in sports

ACT 2

Growing in Circles, Growing in Love

Introduction

The second Act has some important things to tell you about the three circles in our diagram and about God's plan for you and your life.

 Watch Act 2

Father and Son Discussion

For this section, refer to the list of virtues as you go through and answer the questions. The column on the left lists some of the virtues that you are developing in your family love circle. The column on the right shows some of the virtues needed to build good friendships. The middle column represents the virtues needed for you to be who God created YOU to be.

The word "virtue" here is meant to encompass "character strengths." These words describe the many areas of human goodness.

LOVE REQUIRES VIRTUE

FAMILY VIRTUES	PERSONAL VIRTUES	FRIENDSHIP VIRTUES
Respect	Faith	Cooperation
Sharing	Modesty	Humility
Obedience	Good Judgment	Leadership
Caring	Integrity	Fairness
Patience	Compassion	Independence
Forgiveness	Confidence	Trust
Gratitude	Courage	Confidence
Helpfulness	Self-Denial	Honesty
Responsibility	Chastity	Courtesy
Truthfulness	Competence	Teamwork
Kindness	Initiative	Goodness
Courage	Thoughtfulness	Self-Control

1. Ask your Dad to pick three of the virtues in the Family column that he sees you practicing on a daily basis. Have him put a plus sign (+) next to those three and explain why he is picking them.

2. Now, you pick three virtues from the Family column that you know you need to work on more. Mark them with a minus sign (-) and tell your Dad when and how you will try to practice those more often.

3. Next, think about the kids you spend most of your time with. Pick three of them and write down their names. Beside their names, pick one of the virtues from the Friendship column that they practice often. Tell your Dad about a specific time each friend practiced that virtue.

Friend: Charlie   Virtue: trust

Friend: Calben   Virtue: Honesty

Friend: Kade   Virtue: Confidence

4. Ask your Dad to pick three virtues either from the Family column or the Friendship column that he wants you to practice when you're with your friends. Ask him to tell you some examples of how you can practice them.

Virtue Patience

Virtue Leadership

Virtue Forgiveness

5. The Personal Virtues in the center list have to do with you and your efforts to be the unique individual God created you to be. Write down three and tell your Dad the meaning of them and how you can practice them. Then have your Dad pick three more and give his own examples of how you can practice those.

Personal Virtues I want to work on:

Virtue Confidence / Compassion

Virtue Courage / modesty

Virtue Faith / self denial

Personal Virtues Dad suggests that I work on:

Virtue _Compassion_

Virtue _Modesty_

Virtue _Self-denial_

6. The video told us that the virtues are like spiritual muscles we have to exercise every day if we want to be morally strong. We also have to exercise our physical muscles. Let's do that now.

If you are doing this event in a group, wait until the Facilitator tells you all to do this at the same time.

See how many push-ups you can do in one minute. Ask your Dad to keep count.

I can do _____ push-ups in one minute.

80

ACT 3

God's Story . . . From the Beginning

Introduction

Act 3 zooms out to God's view of the universe and helps us learn that everything we are and everything we have is a gift of God's creative love. Watch carefully in the video for some pictures of Bible stories that show God's love.

Watch Act 3

Father and Son Discussion

Listed below are some quotes from the video. Take turns reading them with your Dad and discuss the questions.

1. "God made the whole world, and He made it amazing." Name some of the things in God's world that you think are amazing.

   <u>Family</u>

   <u>Friends</u>

   <u>Shelter</u>

2. "God made fish to swim, animals to run, and planets to circle the sun." What did He make us human beings to do?

   love one another

   care for each other

3. "God gives every human being two great gifts that make us capable of loving—the ability to know and understand (intellect) and the power to make free choices (free will)." In what ways do human beings misuse these gifts?

   Messing around

   littering

4. "Sin is a choice to turn away from God. Sinful choices tear families apart, ruin friendships, and corrupt romantic relationships." Discuss some of the unloving choices that can cause these bad consequences.

5. "When we are children, our parents try to protect us from all harmful things." What are some of the ways your parents have tried to protect you from evil? Ask your Dad to help you think of these ways, and have him explain why he and your Mom did these things.

take us to church

learn our Faith

discipline

6. With your Dad's help, draw lines to match the Bible story with the lesson of God's love. Ask him to talk to you about how each story applies to family life today. If you need help, search for the following passages: Luke 15:11-32, Luke 24, John 19, Luke 10:25-37.

The Prodigal Son

Jesus Christ took the punishment for our sins because He loves us so much.

The resurrection of Jesus

God is a loving Father, and He waits with open arms to forgive us when we are sorry for our sins.

The crucifixion of Jesus

When we are wounded by someone else's sin, God sends someone to bring us the healing power of His love.

The Good Samaritan

God's love is stronger than sin and death. He redeemed us with His great love.

7. Tell your Dad about a recent time you remember seeing love being shared within your family. Ask him to also tell you about a loving family time that he remembers. Write down a few words to describe them, which will help you recall them later.

When we don't argue and fight
When we hug eachother.

8. The video ends by saying: "Now it's our turn to help create a loving world." Name some of the ways you and your family are trying to do this.

going to confession
practicing our faith

Affirming the Good

Dad, you can see that I love God when I

don't argue about going to church
Care for my family

Dad, I can see that you love God when you

When you help me with
things that I struggle with,
Make me food.

ACT 4

Big Changes

Introduction

Act 4 will explain some of the physical and mental changes that occur in your body during the years of puberty.

 Watch Act 4

Father and Son Discussion

1. Review the male anatomy diagram on the next page with your Dad and answer these questions. This will help you learn about the changes going on inside your body. Use the following answer key: A. testicle B. penis, C. scrotum, D. sperm.

   The ___C___ is a soft sac that holds the two testicles just outside of a male body.

   The ___A___ is a small ball-shaped organ that produces male hormones.

   The ___B___ is the male organ through which both urine and semen can pass.

   The ___D___ are the male reproductive cells.

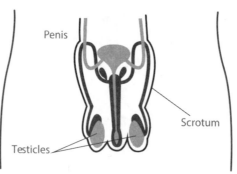

Male Anatomy Diagram

Penis

Scrotum

Testicles

2. Check off the goals below once you accomplish them.

☑ I know the proper names of my body parts.

☐ I can refer to the proper names if necessary without laughing or being embarrassed.

☑ I know that God created the male body to become a father some day (after he is married).

☑ I know that God created a woman's body so that she has the ability to carry a baby and feed it (after she is married).

☐ I know how to respond with virtue when I feel moody.

☐ I understand what is meant by an erection.

☑ I understand what happens in a wet dream (nocturnal emission).

3. Tell your Dad about some ways you like to burn off your extra energy. What games or sports do you enjoy the most? Ask your Dad what his favorite activities were when he was a boy.

4. What changes are already taking place in your body? Check all that apply.

☑ I need to use deodorant.

☐ I am getting hair in new places.

☑ It is more difficult to control my moods.
☑ I get tired more often.
☐ My mustache hair is starting to get darker.
☐ I have wet dreams.
☐ I get spontaneous erections.
☑ I am getting taller.
☑ I am getting smarter.
☐ Other changes I want to tell/ask Dad about

5. It's important to manage your emotions as you mature. Pick at least three emotions that you have experienced recently and draw lines to a virtue that could help you manage it. Explain your choices to your Dad and ask him for help if you need to.

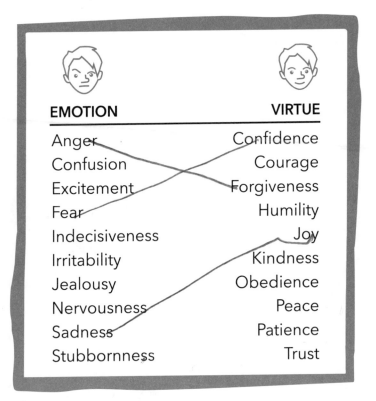

EMOTION	VIRTUE
Anger	Confidence
Confusion	Courage
Excitement	Forgiveness
Fear	Humility
Indecisiveness	Joy
Irritability	Kindness
Jealousy	Obedience
Nervousness	Peace
Sadness	Patience
Stubbornness	Trust

Affirming the Good

Dad, you see me growing into a man when I

Smell your Body odor

Dad, you help me see what it means to be a man when you

love mom,

ACT 5

The Journey towards Love

Introduction

Act 5 helps you learn how to live God's love as a teenager and adult. You will learn some tips on how to become *strong* in your decisions, *smart* in your knowledge of life, and *pure* in your thoughts and actions. Listen for the good news that there are many people who are here to help you along this journey.

 Watch Act 5

Father and Son Discussion

The main goal of *LoveEd* is to help *you* become *smart*, *strong*, and *pure* as you move toward manhood. The next activity will help you review with your Dad how much you have learned.

Understanding Life and Love (with my Intellect)

In order to be *smart* about your manhood, you need to understand many things about life and love. Some of these are listed below. Read each item to your Dad and mark it with one of the following signs:

+ A plus sign means you understand it and accept how important it is. You can use two or three plus signs if you find it especially important. Tell your Dad why.

? A question mark means something about it is still not clear to you.

⊞ God created me for love. As I walk the path of life, God wants me to *learn* to love and to *choose* to love.

⊞ The most important "school" where I am learning how to love is my own family.

⊞ When I truly love someone, I choose what is best for the other person instead of always thinking of what I want for myself.

⊞ It is important for me to choose friends who can help me to practice virtue and become my best self.

⊞ I am learning to love in my family and in my friendship circles by practicing virtues every day— virtues like respect, courage, gratitude, responsibility, forgiveness, honesty, and cooperation.

⊞ The changes in my body that begin at puberty are God's way of preparing me to be a husband and father someday.

⊞ As I move through adolescence, God wants me to develop true friendships with many girls and boys, getting to know them as persons and respecting them as friends.

✠ Someday, when I experience romantic relationships, the virtue of chastity will help me to be pure, to treat the young women I date with love and respect, and to expect them to treat me with respect.

✠ Marriage is a solemn vow to God by which a man and a woman promise to love and care for one another until death and to create a loving family together.

✠ God wants my life to be a *gift of love* either to my future wife and family, to God and the service of the Church, or in generous service to the world as a single person.

Making One Good Choice after Another (with my Free Will)

In order to be spiritually *strong* and *pure*, you need to practice virtue. You acquire virtues by making one good choice after another. Listed below are some *good choices* that will help you become a responsible and loving adult. You can make these choices, with the helping grace of God, as you follow His plan for you to choose real love.

Read each item to your Dad and mark it with one of the following signs:

✝ A plus sign means you understand it and accept how important it is.

❓ A question mark means something about it is still not clear to you.

✠ I will respect my parents and help them to make my family a place where people love and respect one another.

✠ I will ask for—and listen to—my parents' guidance concerning friendships, entertainment, the Internet, and sexuality.

✠ I will choose friends who have positive values and can help me to live up to the virtues my family has taught me.

✠ I will be a good and trusted friend. I will stand up for kids who are being picked on or bullied.

✠ I will be friendly and respectful to girls—talking with them, getting to know them, and doing class assignments and projects with them.

✠ I will avoid using alcohol and drugs—anything that will weaken or destroy my ability to make good choices.

✠ I will avoid pornography—any pictures, shows, songs, texts, or jokes that refer to people's bodies in a disrespectful way.

✠ I will pray every day for the grace to be a loving person in my family and friendship circles and to make good choices that will help me to be morally strong.

✠ I will go to Mass every week and really participate in the prayers and singing.

✠ I will try to remember that Jesus walks with me every minute, always encouraging me to be the best, most loving person I can be.

Now walk through this map with your Dad and review the meaning of each little icon.

Map From the Journey towards Love Video

List one message that struck you as powerful as you watched Act 5:

To love and respect the girls you want to be with.

Affirming the Good

Dad, you see that I am being spiritually strong when I

pray

Dad, you see that I am being smart about my manhood when I

Dad, you see that I am committed to being pure when I

Don't look at bad stuff on the internet

Finish by telling your Dad when he most helps you to become strong, smart, and pure.

When you talk to me about things

Planning Time to be with my Dad

Before you begin the final Act, fill in the following with each other to make a commitment with your Dad to work together on Part II of the program. You will be reading each chapter and answering discussion questions with your Dad.

Dad, let's plan *now* when we will finish Part II of this *LoveEd* program at home.

The best day of the week for us to spend time alone together is ___Sunday___.

The best time of day for us to spend time alone together is _at night_____.

The best place for us to spend time alone together is _in my room_.

Let's plan to do . . .

Chapter 1 on _____ at _____ o'clock

Chapter 2 on _____ at _____ o'clock.

Chapter 3 on _____ at _____ o'clock.

Chapter 4 on _____ at _____ o'clock.

Chapter 5 on _____ at _____ o'clock.

Chapter 6 on _____ at _____ o'clock.

Thanks, Dad!

To complete Part II of the program, you will need to read each chapter before meeting with your Dad.

ACT 6

Prayer and Blessing Ceremony

This final Act in *LoveEd* leads us back to God our Father who loves us. By now we all know that we need God's grace in order to love well. Jesus, as a young adolescent, was determined to follow God's will.

In lieu of a video for Act 6, with fathers and sons together, read and discuss the bible story of Jesus with His parents in the temple at age twelve (Lk 2:41-52). Focus on the last part of the passage that says Jesus was "obedient" to his parents and that he "advanced in wisdom and age and favor before God and man."

Discuss why it is important to always obey your parents, as well as God the Father, in order to grow in wisdom and in grace.

Once your discussion is complete, each father and son will read a prayer of blessing for each other.

A Parent's Blessing

God, our Father and Creator,
You have entrusted to me the life of [name] as a gift from
You.
He is a gift to our family and to the world.
Thank You for him.

As [name] moves through his adolescent years,
may he continue to grow, as young Jesus did,
in wisdom, strength, and grace.

Beloved God, guide him each day
as he makes his life a gift of love,
to You and to all people.
Help [name] be strong, smart, and pure,
and full of faith, hope, and love.

God, I ask Your blessing on my dear son.
Pour out Your grace on him and draw him close to You.
Through Christ our Lord.
Amen.

A Son's Prayer for His Father

God, our Father and Creator,
I thank You for my Dad.
Bless him with Your great love and mercy.
Help him to be the best father he can be:
a man of virtue and strength.
Give him the courage and faith he needs to
teach me and guide me
so that we both may do Your will and create
a more loving world.
Amen.

PART II

At-Home Follow-Up

Once you have completed Part I with your Dad, work through these six chapters. They will help you review the information found in the videos and provide more ideas about educating yourself for real love. Answer the questions after each chapter and discuss your answers with your Dad so he can help you discover practical ways to live these lessons.

CHAPTER 1

What Do I Really Want?

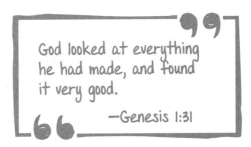

> God looked at everything he had made, and found it very good.
>
> —Genesis 1:31

Joey Sullivan, age eleven, woke up and stared out the upstairs window. His head was filled with the desire for adventure.

Within the house were five other people—the people who made up his family. Two were younger than him: Ava, six, and Alex, six months. The rest were older: Michael, fourteen, who was asleep in the room he shared with Joey, and Mr. and Mrs. Sullivan—mom and dad—who were asleep across the hall.

In front of him, through the window, was the whole world. Some of it he knew—the school, the empty lot, the twenty-four-hour superstore, and the Garcia's house, for instance. Most of it he had not seen and never would see.

He would probably never see the Alps. He would probably never see the Yellow River in China. He would probably never see the view you get when the sun rises behind the earth as you sit in your space capsule and dock with a space station.

He wondered, too, if he would ever see mysteries closer to home: the employees-only section of the twenty-four-hour superstore, the laser room at Kidz Funzone, the Nerf-gun battle park, and "the mystery of womanhood" that his big brother Michael said he learned about at school.

He was thinking a lot about Kidz Funzone because he had been invited to a birthday party there two months ago but had been too sick to go. He was thinking a lot about the "mysteries of womanhood" because thoughts about that kept coming to his mind. But he was thinking a lot about all the places he couldn't go and things he couldn't see because of something the priest said Sunday at Mass.

The priest had read the Gospel story about Jesus sending the disciples out two by two with nothing but the clothes on their backs. He said that the Catholic life was just like that: an adventure that God sends each of us out on.

Joey had paid attention because it seemed like Father Ed was talking specifically to him.

"Did you ever want to go on an adventure?" he asked. Yes, Joey had.

"Did you ever want to be like Bilbo Baggins, an ordinary guy who got called out into a world filled with trolls and goblins to fight, but also dwarves and elves and wizards to help you?" he asked. As a matter of fact, Joey had wanted *exactly* that.

"Did you ever want to be like Princess Elsa from *Frozen* and do great things against great odds?" the priest asked. Joey smiled. He liked that Father Ed was trying to say something for the girls, and he liked that he was kind of getting it wrong. Was Elsa even a princess? And what did she do besides sing "Let It Go"?

"You *can* go on an adventure!" the priest said. "Your whole life can be an adventure! Jesus is sending you on an adventure!"

Joey looked out the window. He wanted to believe the priest, but his life sure didn't feel like an adventure.

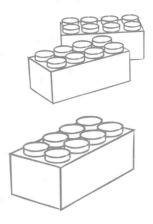

He walked back through his room, past his sleeping brother. He wondered if Michael was dreaming about "the mystery of womanhood."

There were Legos on the floor, so Joey had to watch his step. He liked building with Legos, but he was getting older. He wanted to build with more.

He passed his dad's room. There lay mom and dad, side by side, in bed. His mom was kind of slumped over with her mouth open. Her womanhood didn't look very mysterious at the moment.

Joey focused on his dad. Dad built things. He built the shed out back. He built the deck. He worked for a company that had built offices all over, and he was important there. They called him all the time with questions, sometimes even when he was on vacation, though mom didn't like that.

Dad was just waking up. Baby Alex was stirring in his crib by the bed. His little sister Ava was stretched out sideways at dad's feet. Mr. Sullivan smiled and winked at Joey, putting a finger to his lips to indicate that he should be quiet because mom and Ava were asleep.

Just then, Michael came bursting out of the bedroom.

"Joey, clean up your Legos!" he said angrily, not even trying to be quiet. "Dad, they're all over the floor!"

Now Alex was up and mom was opening her eyes, and dad's smile turned to a frown, but he didn't say anything.

"Clean them up, Joey," dad said.

It seemed like Joey was all alone in the house sometimes.

Joey had to be quiet, but Michael could make all the noise he wanted. Joey could complain about Michael and nothing would happen. Michael could complain about Joey's Legos, and Joey had to fix it.

Joey was too old to go and sleep in mom and dad's room. But he was too young to be treated like Michael was. Whatever this was, it was no adventure.

"Your adventure will take you by surprise," Father Ed had said. "You will see new things you never saw before, face new dangers you never faced before, and discover that you have great abilities, powers, and resources that you never knew you had. God made you, and He knows how much you can do, so He will never ask for too much. But He will also never ask for too little. That is why life is such an adventure."

When he had said what came next, it seemed like Father Ed was practically looking straight at Joey.

"You have a great power, just by being you. Never forget what Peter Parker's uncle told him in Spider-Man: 'With great power comes great responsibility.' You have great power. Use it well."

Those words came back to Joey as he cleaned up the Legos.

With great power comes great responsibility. Dad was responsible for a lot: the cars, the house, the kids, his job. Michael was responsible for a lot: He was getting ready for high school; he had a lawn-mowing business; he had a cell phone; he led all the altar servers.

What was Joey responsible for? Picking up Legos. And cleaning up Legos was as far from an adventure as you could get.

"With not-so-great power comes not-so-great responsibility," said Joey out loud.

Suddenly Joey took a handful of Legos and threw them across the room. He ran over to the window.

He wanted more out of life. He wanted to be strong like Michael or his dad. He wanted to have cool friends that everyone liked. He wanted to do something amazing and important. He ran downstairs.

"Where's Michael?" he asked his dad, who was holding the baby in one arm and pouring coffee with the other.

"He's going on a bike ride," said Mr. Sullivan.

That's an adventure. Kind of.

"Can I go?" asked Joey.

His dad answered by pointing at the trash, which was overflowing its bin.

"That trash is my great responsibility," said Joey with a sardonic grin. "Then can I go?"

His dad looked puzzled at the first comment, but nodded.

Three minutes later Joey and Michael were racing down their quiet neighborhood street, coming up on the vacant lot.

"Michael, do you really believe what Father Ed said?" Joey asked.

"What did Father Ed say?"

"You know, about life being an adventure."

"I'll show you an adventure," said Michael, and he pedaled quickly away across the empty lot toward the Garcia's house.

"You're just chasing the mystery of womanhood!" teased Joey. "The mystery of *Julia.*" He said Julia Garcia's name with a mocking tone, then turned sharply and went around the street to cut Michael off.

He found Michael parked by the side of the road, checking his phone. He looked at the screen and scowled.

"I really wish you would tell your friends that I'm not your secretary," Michael said.

"Hey, it's not my fault that mom and dad won't let me have my own phone," said Joey.

Michael handed the phone to him. It was a text from Joey's friend Rob. "Does Joey want to hang out?" it said.

Joey was starting to text a response when Michael's friend, Greg, zoomed past on his bike. He grabbed the phone from Joey.

"Give it back!" said Joey as Greg raced ahead. Greg grinned and typed a response to Rob: "No one likes you, Rob."

Joey caught up with him and grabbed the phone back.

"Sorry. Joey here. That wasn't me," he texted Rob.

Joey turned red with embarrassment. He didn't know what to do to handle these friend problems. He knew Greg could be mean sometimes, but he also knew that Rob could act goofy sometimes.

"What the heck, Greg?" shouted Michael.

"I was just joking," he said. "You guys have no sense of humor. And you've got goofy little friends. And you're slow!

Last one to the stop sign is a total loser!"

Greg took off in a blaze of speed, and Michael and Joey followed. Joey was side by side with them at first, but then he started breathing heavily and slipping further and further behind. Michael stopped to wait for him.

"Loser, loser, Joey is a loser!" taunted Greg.

"Knock it off, will you?" said Michael. "Hey bro, don't pay attention to him. He's just goofing around," he said to Joey.

Michael's phone buzzed. Joey glanced at it. It was Julia Garcia texting Michael.

"Hey there," is all it said. But Joey knew that it would be a very important message to Michael.

"Here's your Mystery of Womanhood," said Joey, handing Michael his phone and then riding away.

"Joey, come on," said Michael. "Come back!"

But then Michael read the text and stopped paying attention to Joey and Greg altogether. He was texting back and forth with Julia, oblivious to all else.

Joey ignored him back. He rode home and found his dad walking the dog along the sidewalk.

"Joey, you didn't do a very thorough job with those Legos," his dad said. Then, seeing that Joey was upset, he said, "Come on, buddy, help me take Duke for a walk."

Joey didn't answer, but he didn't get off his bike, either.

"Did you and Michael get in a fight?"

"No . . ." Joey replied.

"Come on, buddy, give me a hint. What's wrong?"

Joey stared up at his bedroom window but didn't answer.

"When is Rob coming over?" asked Mr. Sullivan.

"He's not."

"Didn't he text you on Michael's phone? He said he would when he called here."

"Yeah, but I don't want him to come over," said Joey.

"Why not?"

"I don't know. Rob is kind of goofy."

"Goofy? What are you talking about? You guys have been best friends forever."

"I don't know. That's what everyone else says."

"Did your brother say Rob is goofy?" asked Mr. Sullivan.

"No," Joey replied.

"Joey, did Greg say that?"

Joey's silence answered the question for him.

"Well, if your brother doesn't think he's goofy and your dad doesn't think he's goofy, what does it matter what Greg thinks? Maybe Rob just needs someone to stick up for him. Maybe that someone is you! One day you're going to be a man, and if you want to be a man, you have to look out for others and protect people that are being picked on."

"But . . . he's just a kid, Dad. He only wants to do kid stuff. I want to grow up. I want to do more."

"Well, you're just a kid, too," answered Mr. Sullivan. "I mean, there's nothing wrong with being a kid. You may feel small now, but you've got a big heart, and if you take a stand for doing what's right, you might surprise yourself at how big of an effect you can have. So why don't you invite Rob over and make your old man proud?"

Joey stared straight ahead, sullenly. But he nodded.

"Is something else bothering you?" Joey's dad asked him.

Joey was quiet, and then spoke in a burst, "I'm just sick of being just a kid. Life is supposed to be an adventure. My life isn't an adventure. I want to build with more than Legos. I want to go faster on my bike. I want to see more than I can see out of my bedroom window. I don't have any big powers, I don't have any responsibilities, and I don't even know what the Mystery of Womanhood even means." Then

Joey added as an afterthought, "I also want to go to Kidz Funzone, by the way."

Mr. Sullivan smiled. "I see what's bothering you. And I think it's time we had a little talk."

Duke barked as if he understood, too.

Discussion Questions

Answer and discuss these questions with your Dad.

1. What do you sometimes think about when you daydream?

2. What are the three most fun and exciting places you have been?

3. Father Ed said that Catholic life was like an adventure. What is your favorite adventure story? How has your life been an adventure so far?

4. What has been tough for you to do or get through in your life? Who or what helped you get stronger to get through it?

_____

_____

_____

Chapter Reflections

While discussing this chapter, my Dad gave me some extra advice about . . .

_____

_____

_____

While reading this chapter, I learned these two important things:

1. _____

2. _____

I resolve to live out the *LoveEd* teachings from this chapter by . . .

_____

_____

_____

Finish this chapter with the following prayer:

Lord, thank You for my family and my friends. Thank You for the good times and the bad. Help us all to love one another as You love us. Amen.

My Dad and I completed this chapter on

_____

(date and time)

CHAPTER 2

Getting Stronger All the Time

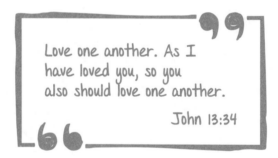

> Love one another. As I
> have loved you, so you
> also should love one another.
>
> John 13:34

"Let's go up to your bedroom," said Mr. Sullivan. "I'll put Duke in the yard and meet you there."

Joey went into the house. He was putting the last Legos away as his dad walked in. Here is what Mr. Sullivan told him:

"This bedroom is your bedroom, but it could just as easily be anyone else's.

"Human beings are special in a way things and places aren't. I love this bedroom because it is your bedroom. About eleven years ago, God decided to create you, Joseph Andrew Sullivan, and you are what makes this place special.

"There are millions of bedrooms in the world almost exactly like this one, but there is only one you.

"God made no other you. He made only one person who looks exactly like you, thinks exactly likes you, and has the exact talents you have. God looked at the whole world and the whole plan of history and He saw one thing missing—you—and so He filled in that gap. Your mom and I were glad to help him out.

"God wanted someone with your color hair, your height, your size, someone with your ability to look at problems and fix them. He wanted someone who would try to build things the way you do. He wanted someone who is as happy as you are when they get to spend time with his friends. God wanted someone who is smart but not a show-off, someone who is good at sports but tries to include others, and He knew just the guy: you.

"He wanted someone as loyal to his friends as you have always been, Joey.

"He wanted someone who would stare out that window and remember a priest's homily and ask questions about it. Not many people do that, Joey.

"But you have great questions—and you only get the big answers by asking the great questions. Look out the window. Imagine for a minute where we are. We are in a far corner of the Milky Way galaxy on a planet that's spinning in circles around the sun.

"I want you to think about our solar system for a minute. It's made up of eight or nine planets—I know you have your own opinions about Pluto. Each planet is a giant chunk of rock hurling through space in an orbit so regular that scientists can predict where each one will be twenty years from now.

"They all spin around the sun, a star so bright that it

lights up every one of them.

"God made the sun and the planets, too, but what do you think is greater: those planets or Joseph Andrew Sullivan?

"I know which is greater. Those planets go in predictable circles, but no one knows where Joey will go next. No scientist, even with all the data about you and all the computer power in the world, could predict where you will be twenty years from now.

"And what about that bright sun that gives us all our sunny days and even lights up the night through the moon? That sun lights up every tree on this block, but it can't tell you anything about them. The sun lights up the moon, but the sun knows nothing about the moon. That sun is just a big ball of burning gasses that will one day die out. You, Joseph Andrew Sullivan, have seen more than the sun has seen, and you know infinitely more than the sun.

"That's why you're great.

"You're great because God gave you free will—the ability to choose where you want to go and who you want to be and how you want to give glory to God. The planets can't choose; you can.

"You're also great because in addition to free will, God gave you your intellect—the ability to know things. You don't just shine like the sun. You don't just see things like a bird. You know things. You can figure out what is true and what is not true. You can figure out what is good and what is not good. You can appreciate what is beautiful and remember it and tell someone else about it.

"Why did God create you?

"You know the answer: God created you to know Him with your intellect, love Him with your free will, and be happy with Him forever. God has a plan for teaching you to love and for helping you to become the unique and special person that is you. But what, really, is love? Love is sacrificing yourself for the good of others.

"God's plan for love can be represented by three circles. These circles are actually found within an even greater circle: the circle of God's love, which surrounds and gives grace to these three circles that you are (or will be) a part of in your life. The first circle is family love—where you learn to be a loving member of your family. The second is friendship love—where you learn to be a faithful friend. You are already called to exercise your special powers of choosing and knowing in both these circles. But there is another circle you have not been called to yet: the circle of romantic love.

"Romantic love won't be a big part of your life for several years now, but I want you to start thinking about it because your body is already beginning to prepare for it. As you grow up, God wants you to learn how to receive love and how to respond by loving back in each of these three circles.

"According to God's plan, you will spend your life moving from one circle to another. And again, all of it happens within that larger circle—the circle of God's love. But it isn't like the planets. They are stuck in their circle around the sun. But you can choose where you go and how you go about things in your circle.

"Let's look at each circle . . .

The Family Circle

"The first and most important circle is the family. Family love begins even before you're born. The minute your parents know of your existence, they begin to surround you with a world of love. And as you grow up, they care for you every day. They share your joys and struggles and teach you the difference between right and wrong.

"In addition to your parents, brothers, and sisters, the family love circle includes your grandparents, aunts, uncles, cousins, and other close family friends who care for you. Your role in the family circle is to learn, at every stage of your life, how to love in return all of the people who love you.

FAMILY

"God wants every child he creates to be brought up in a loving family circle where he or she will be loved and cared for at every minute. It doesn't always work that way though, does it? We know that every family has its challenges: Some are single-parent families, some are blended families, and even those families with parents still married to each other don't always agree on every issue. Some families do not have children, some have children with disabilities, some have children they were blessed to adopt, and some have children that don't live with them. Yet, in each of our families, we learn to love in our own unique situation according to God's plan.

"Learning to love means developing personal strengths we call virtues. In family life, you see the importance of virtues such as kindness, patience, truthfulness, and forgiveness, and you begin to make them your own. But the virtues can be thought of as spiritual muscles. You have to exercise them until they become part of *you*. These 'building blocks' of virtue also include fortitude, honesty, faithfulness, and obedience. Other virtues can help you resist temptation, such as self-control, diligence, and perseverance. There are some unique features about family love. For instance, you don't have to earn it. Your family loves you just because you are family, not because you are good or beautiful or talented. But you do have to learn how to love them back."

Mr. Sullivan stopped and looked deep into his son's eyes.

"Joey, you know how very much we all love you, right?"

Joey smiled and nodded, and soon his dad was telling him about the second circle.

The Friendship Circle

"The second circle represents the kind of love we call friend-ship. In this circle you have to learn to love people outside your family, people who don't already love you.

"Once you start school, and sometimes a little before, you move into the friendship circle. You don't choose your parents or your siblings, but you do choose your friends. You also choose how you act, where you go, and what you do when you're with your friends.

"Friendship is different than family love in other ways. For example, you *do* have to earn friendship. Friendship love doesn't come automatically. If you want to have friends, you have to *be* a friend. You have to learn how to make and keep friends. There are ways you have to act if you want other kids to like you. You know there are things you should do and not do in the friendship circle.

"But friendship gives you the chance to use the virtues

you have been practicing in your family. Here you can also learn new virtues like teamwork, leadership, cooperation, trust, independence, and sticking up for yourself and others. You also have to learn loyalty. You have to learn to be faithful to your friends in all things that don't involve sin.

Expanding Your Friendship Circle

"The people around us outside of our family circle may become more important to us during puberty and adolescence. You may want to go over to your friends' houses more often or have friends over. You may admire your teachers and want to stay after school or help them before school. You might sometimes enjoy being at school more than being at home because it's fun and new. You may also find new role models in your coaches, pastors, or youth ministers; you might even find qualities you admire in certain famous athletes, singers, and movie stars.

"At this stage of life, you begin to look around and see where you fit into society. You ask yourself, 'Where do I belong in this big world outside my family? In whose footsteps do I follow? What talents or gifts do I have to offer? What can I do to make the world a better place for others?'

"Your preteen and teenage years are an important time to explore the circle of friendship. Whether you're at school, in church, or playing at the park or in your neighborhood, you are in the presence of other boys and girls who can become your friends. Good friends know how to play fair and take turns. Good friends listen rather than talk too much. Good friends tell the truth and stick up for others. Good friends are polite to adults and respectful of teachers and pastors. These are qualities of a good friend. When you find friends who share your values and love God, they can help you become the best person you can be.

"Good Christian friends can help you know yourself and

know God better. Choose friends who are also striving to live according to God's plan. A true friend will help lead you to God, not to sin. In life, it's easier to do the right thing if your friend is standing next to you, supporting your good decision. You should do the same for your friends.

"The more you leave the family circle for the friendship circle, you will find that love is not as easy to earn. At home, you know your parents will love you no matter what. But outside your family, in clubs and sports or in school, you need to learn how to earn the love of others. New social skills are not as hard as learning math or science or history, but they do come easily for some people and not so easily for others.

Choose Friends and Role Models Who Lead You to Do Good

"Even as a preteen, there are plenty of choices to make, and they need to be made on what is *right* and *good*, not on how you *feel*. For example, what if your friends want to play a video game that may be indecent or offends God? Do you have the courage to ask them to choose something else? What if some of your friends want to look at immodest pictures? Are you strong enough on the inside to suggest they do something else? What if you're watching TV and something indecent comes on the screen? A sign of Christian maturity would be for you to change the channel or suggest something else to do that's better for you. No matter what you're feeling or how much you want to please your friends, practice doing the right thing and become a true leader for goodness and virtue. Good choices will help you attract more friends who are good, too.

"Many of the role models in popular entertainment today are leading people away from God rather than toward Him. What famous person do you admire? Look around for role models who love God with their whole heart, mind, and soul. You may find good role models more easily in your parents and grandparents than among the rich and famous. If you get involved in your youth group at church, you may also find more friends and role models there as well.

Give Yourself to Others in Need

"God created us to love. Puberty and adolescence is the time to grow out of the selfishness of a needy child into a selfless adult so you will be capable of doing good for others. Practice being more patient, kind, thoughtful, and helpful. Try to be more considerate of elderly people and those in need who can use your help, enthusiasm, and youthful energy. These virtuous acts will help you grow in maturity of mind while your body grows into the mature person God wants you to be.

"Think about it: Are you leading those around you to be better people? Are you leading others to God by your good example? One of the wonderful things about growing up is widening your friendship circle to include all kinds of people. Usually your friends are very much like you, but they don't have to be. Your friends may be taller, shorter, fatter or thinner, sillier, smarter, a different skin color, a different religion, a teacher or coach, an elderly person, a little child, or someone who is handicapped in some way. Sometimes you'll make friends with a girl—but a friend is different than a girlfriend.

The Romance Circle

"And that brings us to the third circle: romantic love. As you enter your teenage years, you will find yourself being attracted to girls, wanting them to notice you and like you. And then as you get older, you may want to have a romantic relationship with a girl you have become friends with.

"The romantic love circle is all about a whole different kind of love—that mysterious process by which two people fall in love, decide to get married, and begin to create a new family love circle.

"This is the 'Mystery of Manhood and Womanhood.' It is something you have not had to think much about yet, but the time will come! At your age, you need to prepare for the upcoming changes of puberty. That is the time in your physical development when your body will start to change from a boy to a man.

"Romantic attraction is also a part of God's plan. During puberty, God prepares your body to be a husband and dad someday. But preparing your mind and heart? That's another major process. It will take you ten years or more to develop the virtues you will need to be a loving husband and father.

"Eventually, most people will fall in love. You will find a young woman you love and care about so deeply that you will want to spend your whole lifetime with her. Or you may come to realize that God is calling you to give your life to Him as a priest or religious brother. If you're called to be a priest or religious brother, you will spend your life bringing God's love and care into the lives of others.

"I'll be delighted with either plan, Joey! I would love seeing you as a husband and father or as a priest, religious brother, or consecrated single person. But I know most about God's calling to be a loving husband and father—because that's what He chose for me. If you're like me, you will have a wedding someday, and we'll gather all the people you love—everyone from your family circle and your friendship circle—to celebrate your marriage.

"On that special day, you and the woman you love will stand before God and solemnly promise that you will love one another until death. After your wedding, you will start a family of your own. And then your children will begin to journey through the love circles, following their own path from family love, to friendship, to romance and a new family.

"But whatever plan God has for your future, your task is to become a responsible, loving person in the two circles where you live *now*—your family circle and your friendship circle. You become a loving person by developing *virtues*. To develop these virtues, you have to make one good choice after another. You have to choose to be kind, choose to be patient, choose to be truthful, and choose to be forgiving.

"Friendship gives you the chance to use the virtues you've learned in your family. Your friendship group needs the positive values and attitudes that your family has taught you.

"You have to practice the family and friendship virtues over and over until they become part of *you*.

"Later, when you're ready to step into the circle of romantic love, you will need those spiritual muscles you have been working on more than ever. In all of your relationships with young women, you will need to practice virtues like kindness, respect, self-control, honesty, and truthfulness. And there is a special virtue that God wants you to pray for and work on starting now. It's called chastity. Chastity is the virtue that directs our manhood toward authentic love and away from using people. By practicing chastity, you are being faithful to your future wife even before you meet her!

"So what about *now*? Your job *now* is to respond to God's love for you by being the best *you* you can be, by being a loving member of your family, and by being a strong and trustworthy friend.

"God has a special plan for each one of us, and that plan is to be a gift of love. God has a plan for teaching you to love—and to learn to be the unique and special person that is *you*.

"God created you so that He could love you forever. God wants you to learn to love Him back."

Mr. Sullivan stopped and approached Joey, who had been sitting by the window and looking through the clear panes.

"You can stop looking out the window now, by the way," Mr. Sullivan said, giving Joey a big hug. "There's a lot more to talk about. But first, I want you to do one thing for me."

"What is it, Dad?" asked Joey.

"Pick the Lego off the windowsill, please," he said with a smile. "Someone must have thrown it there."

Discussion Questions

Answer and discuss these questions with your Dad.

1. Why did God make you? Try to remember the answer from the story, or maybe you learned it in religion class before this.

_____

_____

_____

2. What is the earliest memory you have of your family? What does this memory tell you about family love?

_____

_____

_____

3. What does your Mom rely on your Dad to do for the family? What does your Dad rely on your Mom to do?

_____

_____

_____

4. Who was your first friend? How are your friendships different now?

_____

_____

_____

5. What story, from any book or movie or from real life, best captures for you the meaning of a true friend?

_____

_____

_____

6. How strong are your friendships?

Name three of your friends.

_____

_____

_____

What do you like about each of them?

_____

_____

_____

Name three qualities that make you a good friend to others.

_____

_____

_____

Who could be your friend if you reached out more?

_____

_____

_____

How can you better get along with different types of people?

_____

_____

_____

What friends are your best role models, and how do they lead you to do good?

_____

_____

_____

Chapter Reflections

While discussing this chapter, my Dad gave me some extra advice about . . .

_____

_____

_____

While reading this chapter, I learned these two important things:

1. _____

2. _____

I resolve to live out the _LoveEd_ teachings from this chapter by . . .

_____

_____

_____

Finish this chapter with the following prayer:
Lord, thank You for my family and my friends. Thank You for the good times and the bad. Help us all to love one another as You love us. Amen.

My Dad and I completed this chapter on

_____

(date and time)

CHAPTER 3

Becoming a Man for Family and Friends

> For God so loved the world that he gave his only Son, so that everyone who believes in him might not perish but might have eternal life.
>
> John 3:16

"Let's review the circles of life we've talked about so far," said Joey's dad. "What are the circles?"

"The family circle, the friend circle, and the circle of romantic love," answered Joey.

"Very good!" said Mr. Sullivan. "You're a boy now. What will puberty change your body into?"

"A man!"

Mr. Sullivan laughed. "Very good, Joey. The bottom line is that puberty is about you becoming a man. We're going to talk next about how to be a man in the family and friendship circles because you need to be a man at home and with your friends before you can even think about being a man who enters the romantic circle. I was inspired to be like Roger Donlon, a true man, when he spoke at my school. Do you mind if I tell you about him?"

"Sure," answered Joey.

And so Mr. Sullivan told Joey about Roger Donlon. But first he explained that the Medal of Honor is the United States of America's highest military honor, awarded for personal acts of valor above and beyond the call of duty. Joey's dad said that Colonel Roger Donlon was the first soldier to be awarded the Medal of Honor in the Vietnam War, and the first member of the US Army Green Berets to receive the honor.

On July 6, 1964, Col. Donlon was with his men at camp when a much larger enemy battalion attacked them in the darkness. After the first attack, Donlon got his men together and noticed that the ammunition was in danger of being burned and the camp's gate was unprotected.

He ran to the gate, despite enemy bullets and grenades, and stopped the enemies who were about to blow it up. A bullet hit his stomach, but he didn't let that stop him. He saw a sergeant in trouble and dragged him to safety. That's when an enemy mortar exploded and wounded his left shoulder.

He began saving the ammunition, starting with a large gun. He brought it to a new location where he found three of his men wounded. He administered first aid to them, gave them the weapon, and then started gathering the rest of the ammunition that was in danger.

After that, he crawled 575 feet to another firing position and directed efforts to protect the camp. When he saw the enemy weakening, he left his sheltered position and moved from position to position around the camp, throwing grenades and inspiring his men to keep up the fight. As he did this, another mortar shell wounded him in the face and body.

As daylight broke, the enemy retreated back into the jungle, and the wounded colonel reorganized his defenses and administered first aid to his soldiers.

With fewer than one hundred men, he held off an attacking force of eight hundred to nine hundred enemy attackers for more than five hours in the dead of night. Even though he was wounded repeatedly, he continued to fight and protect his men.

His citation read, "Capt. Donlon's extraordinary heroism, at the risk of his life above and beyond the call of duty, are in the highest traditions of the US Army and reflect great credit upon himself and the Armed Forces of his country."

Just watching Donlon receive the medal, standing straight and courageous, inspired people all across the nation to start being more strong, smart, and pure themselves.

"That's why my teacher invited him to talk to us," said Mr. Sullivan. "Roger Donlon told us that everything he did that night came from who he was at home growing up. He was the eighth of ten children. He learned honesty, integrity, hard work, and personal commitment from his mom and dad. As a young man, he deliberately guided his life by the principles of the Ten Commandments and the Catechism he learned in religion class.

"He told us to pray the Rosary every day, and he shared with us a quote he always keeps with him. It was his wife's favorite quote: 'What we are is God's gift to us. What we become is our gift to God.'

"Ever since I heard him, I wanted to be like him. And I made that my motto: 'What I am is God's gift to me. What I become is my gift back to God.'

"Those are words to live by. Now, that's Roger Donlon's story. But I have one more story to share with you. This is an even 'bigger story' because it's the story of all of us—and it's the greatest adventure story you'll ever hear about. Are you ready, Joey?"

"Of course I am, Dad, I'm always ready for an adventure!"

The Story of Us

Mr. Sullivan began again.

"Life is an adventure that began long before you were born. Before your parents and your grandparents. Before Abe Lincoln and George Washington. Before Joan of Arc and Shakespeare. Before Homer, the Vikings, and cavemen.

"Before anything existed . . . there was God. God made the whole world, and He made it amazing. He filled the sky full of stars. He made snow fall on mountaintops that soar above the clouds. He made oceans and rushing rivers and forests of giant trees. God is the ultimate scientist, writing the laws of the universe. And God is the ultimate artist, setting the standard for beauty.

"The world He made was big and beautiful, but it wasn't enough for Him. God wanted to share His life and love even more. So He made us. We are God's greatest idea, God's artistic masterpiece. Our bodies and souls, our hearts and minds—they're all a reflection of God's greater being.

"Our whole purpose for being is to love one another and give our lives back to the God who gave us everything—everything we are, everything we see. God gives every human being two great gifts that make us capable of loving: the ability to know and understand our intellect, and the power to make free choices, known as our free will.

"He took a great risk in giving us so much power. He knew we could choose to use our freedom and intelligence for Him—or against Him. And right from the beginning, the human race failed to follow God's plan. With our ability to know, we said that we knew better and challenged God's plan. With our power to choose, we chose our own selfish desires and rejected God's love.

"This is the reality we call sin. Sin is a choice to turn away from God. Sin goes against the beauty and order of God's creation because whenever we choose not to follow God's plan, we choose not to love. Our unloving choices have bad consequences for ourselves—and for everyone around us.

"When we're children, our parents try to protect us from all harm. But they can't protect us forever. The older we get, the more temptations we face. We need a lot of courage to resist the pressure to sin and a lot of grace each day to choose to do what is right.

"This leads us to the Devil's broken promises, Joey," his dad said gravely.

"Pope Francis spoke of that choice when he visited South America and told a group of young people about a famous meditation by St. Ignatius on two standards: the standard of the Devil and the standard of Christ.

"'It would be like the football jerseys of two different teams,' said Pope Francis. 'And he asks us which team we want to play for. The Devil, in order to recruit players, promises that those who play on his side will receive riches, honor, glory, and power. They will be famous. Everyone will worship them. But Jesus is different,' Pope Francis told the crowd. 'Jesus doesn't tell us that we will be stars or celebrities in this life. Instead, he tells us that playing with him is about humility, love, and service to others. Jesus does not lie to us; He takes us seriously.'

"The Holy Father described what the Devil tries to do.

"'In the Bible, the Devil is called the father of lies. What he promises, or better, what he makes you think, is that if you do certain things, you will be happy. And later, when you think about it, you realize that you weren't happy at all. That you were up against something which, far from giving you happiness, made you feel more empty, even sad.'

"Francis called the Devil a 'con artist—a liar who only succeeds by fooling people.'

"'He makes promise after promise, but he never delivers,' said the pope. 'He'll never really do anything he says. He doesn't make good on his promises. He makes you want things which he can't give, whether you get them or not. He makes you put your hopes in things which will never make you happy. That's his game, his strategy. He talks a lot; he offers a lot, but he doesn't deliver.'

"Jesus has a different approach. 'He doesn't con us, nor does He promise us the world. He doesn't tell us that we will find happiness in wealth, power, and pride. Just the opposite. He shows us a different way. This coach tells his players, "Blessed, happy are the poor in spirit, those who mourn, the meek, those who hunger and thirst for righteousness, the merciful, the pure in heart, the peacemakers, those who are persecuted for righteousness' sake." And He ends up by telling them, "Rejoice on account of all this!"'"

Joey's dad chuckled. "You're probably wondering why you should be on Jesus' team."

"Yes, maybe a little, when you put it that way," Joey admitted.

"The pope answered that question this way: 'Because Jesus doesn't lie to us. He shows us a path that is life and truth. He is the great proof of this. His style, His way of living, is friendship, relationship with His Father. And that is what He offers us. He makes us realize that we are sons and daughters.'

"The Devil lies about a lot of things, but he especially likes to lie about the circle of romantic love. He has been lying about it for a long time.

"In the beginning, when God created Adam and Eve, God's plan was perfect. Marriage and family were designed to be fulfilling for men, women, and their children. It was designed so that everyone would be happy with each other and in perfect union with God. Something happened that changed that perfect life: an act of disobedience performed through free will—the original sin of Adam and Eve.

"Man and woman fell for Satan's lies. 'You will be like God,' the Devil said. After they committed original sin, their perfect life was wounded and would never be the same. They no longer lived in harmony and selfless love; they became confused about the nature and purpose of their bodies, and they were tempted to use one another out of selfishness.

"After original sin, people actually like to sin rather than to be with God; this is why God knew we needed a savior.

"But here's the rest of the story," Joey's dad continued.

"Out of His mercy and love, God sent His Son, Jesus Christ, to make up for Adam and Eve's sin and for all of our sins so we can live in peace and harmony when we follow His way of love and live a moral life. God's perfect plan was broken by original sin and redeemed by Jesus Christ. Jesus came to earth to show us what God's love is like. And when Jesus died for us, He showed us the ultimate act of love. He taught us that love is always greater than our sin. It's through this love that God redeemed creation.

"Jesus made all things new again. God never stops loving us. God never gives up. When we sin, God always gives us another chance to come home to Him and ask for forgiveness. When we're wounded by another person's sin, God sends someone to bring us the healing power of His love. And when we're confronted by painful situations, we always have the power to choose to love.

"And now it is our turn, Joey. Now it's up to us to bring forth God's love—to overcome sin and to create a loving world."

Strong, Smart, and Pure

Mr. Sullivan went on.

"If I recall, Father Ed said your life is an adventure. You might not be called on to be a heroic man today or tomorrow. But you need to start acting like an everyday hero today and tomorrow and the next day if you're to grow into a heroic man later on. Great men started out by living by a code when they were your age—everyone from George Washington to Roger Donlon. And all of their codes could be boiled down to three points: being strong, smart, and pure.

"Why strong? Look at Roger Donlon. He had to be physically strong to keep going through all those wounds. But he also had to be emotionally strong to be able to keep calm and collected as he fought his attackers at night. He had to be morally strong so he would make clear decisions to do good for others and not compromise his responsibilities, even in the heat of battle. He also had to be spiritually strong in order to have enough hope in his heart that he could trust in God and carry on.

"Why smart? Roger Donlon had to know quite a bit to do what he did. He had to know what his camp needed. He had to know where the ammunition was kept and what the enemy was likely to do. He had to know whom he could count on and where to direct his men. It took a lot of studying and careful planning to be able to do what he did in the dark.

"And why pure? God wants you to see the true value of the people you meet and treat them accordingly. Those with a pure heart fight for the people around them; they never give up on them or use them or choose themselves over others—and when you have a pure heart, the people around you respect and admire you. If a lesser man were guarding that camp, the story could have ended tragically.

"Let's talk about how you can practice each one," Mr. Sullivan said.

Be Strong

"During puberty, it's normal to experience many strong emotions that are both positive and negative. How should you respond? By being strong!

"Some feelings may be great. You may enjoy the feelings of excitement, playfulness, attractiveness, confidence, and satisfaction. Other emotions may be negative or painful—sadness, discouragement, rejection, frustration, or crankiness. Feeling 'blue' or irritable can drag you down if you let it. You may find yourself changing moods more often during puberty than you used to. Sometimes you won't even know why you feel the way you do.

"All negative feelings do not have to be acted out, but it's not good to bury them or stuff them inside, either. We can learn to manage and accept our feelings for what they are—merely indicators of pleasure or pain. Then, when we feel them, the next thing we do is *think*: 'How should I act in response to these feelings that would help myself and others?' Then pray, 'How would God want me to act?' You can use your mind and your free will to practice managing your feelings in many new, more grown-up ways. You may know a two-year-old who throws tantrums when he is mad or frustrated. Now that you're older, you should feel, think, and then act in the most loving way possible. *Feel, think, pray*, then *act*.

"When you go swimming in the ocean, you quickly learn that sometimes the waves and currents can become large and powerful. If you want to swim back to the beach, you have to work hard against the choppy waters. This takes perseverance, especially when you feel too tired to kick your legs and move your arms. Your emotions during puberty may feel like the vigorous waves of the ocean—so strong you feel you can't push back! But just as you must tell yourself to swim back to the beach, you can also tell yourself to swim against the powerful emotions washing over you! But you're strong, too. You can overcome negative emotions by making a decision in your mind and your will.

"Now, let's talk about how you can be smart."

Be Smart

"You're most likely thinking the same things we humans always think about when we enter puberty and adolescence. In fact, we never stop thinking about them: *Why did God make us? Where do we fit in this universe? How do we grow up to be like Jesus and with God?*

"As you learn more in school, at church, and in life, you may begin to think new and different thoughts. You may start to wonder about the meaning of life and your purpose in life. You might start thinking more about what you will do when you grow up. You wonder if you will be married someday and become a dad. You may start asking more questions about everything. You may start looking outside your family for friends and role models. This is all a normal and good part of the growing up process. Remember that we, your parents, were once your age. We had the same questions, thoughts, and doubts that you have. Our wisdom and experience can help guide you through the mental changes of puberty. God also gave you extended family, teachers, and pastors. Along with us, other family members, teachers, and your Church will help you find the right answers you need. So don't be afraid to ask, Joey!

"Now, let's talk about how you can be pure."

Be Pure

"To be pure at heart means to see the true value of those around you. People always said that when St. John Paul II or

St. Teresa of Calcutta looked at them, they felt special. They felt like they were the only people in the world. That's purity of heart. Holy people have a way of seeing how important everyone they meet really is. When you meet someone holy, that person makes you understand not just how good he or she is but also how good you are, too.

"We all need to be pure at heart. You need to see the people in your family as important and worth your best. You need to think of your friends and the people you meet at school as special people, deserving the best you can give them. And you need to see young women as important, special individuals who should be respected and treated kindly. A pure person would never use someone else for his or her own pleasure or gain, and a pure person always tries to help others.

"How can you learn to be smart, strong, and pure in your family circle and friend circle? How can you learn to be a man? Well, let me give you some ideas, son.

How to Make a Man

"The building blocks for manhood are the virtues. If you build these now, you'll be a great man later. If you ignore them, you'll have a much more difficult time in life.

"You will be challenged daily to choose virtues that reflect God's great love or to choose vices such as dishonesty, meanness, disobedience, impurity, or laziness that open the door to evil.

"It's your job right now, as a growing young man, to practice building your character and virtue each day so you can become the man God wants you to be. You will need years of practicing courtesy and respect for others in order to be a good husband and father, priest, or single man.

"The four fundamental virtues are called the cardinal

virtues—practicing these virtues lays the foundation for all the others. They are:

- **Prudence** is being cautious and thinking before you speak and act. It will help you avoid getting caught in a sticky situation that will lead you to sin.

- **Justice** is doing what's right and fair, giving to God what is owed to Him and to others what they are due. It means being truthful with your parents, fair with your friends, and honest with yourself.

- **Fortitude** is having the 'guts' to say *no* to something you know is wrong. It's having the courage to resist evil and do good. It's the mental and emotional strength necessary to face and combat difficulty, adversity, danger, or temptation.

- **Temperance** is a very practical virtue that helps you balance your life using moderation. It's having self-restraint in actions, such as speaking, eating, drinking, or playing. Temperance is all about using self-control. It helps you train your will to win over your impulses and feelings so you turn all your desires toward what is good—no matter what you 'feel' like doing.

"These cardinal virtues help you get on the track to happiness and real love. Practice these well—you'll be glad you did!"

Discussion Questions

Answer and discuss these questions with your Dad.

1. Let's see how strong you are physically:

How many jumping jacks can you do in one minute?

How many sit-ups?

_____

How long can you do yard work?

_____

How long can you play soccer before you have to take a break?

_____

What's the longest hike you have taken?

_____

Now ask your Dad, how does physical training help us become stronger in our mind and will?

_____

_____

2. Consider your own personal strengths and those of your parents':

What do you do well?

_____

_____

What does your Dad do well?

_____

_____

What does your Mom do well?

_____

_____

What can you learn from them?

_____

_____

3. Now consider your behavioral strengths and weaknesses:

What struggles do you have in trying to behave with your brothers and sisters?

_____

_____

What good behaviors do you have toward your brothers or sisters?

_____

_____

When is it hard to do the right thing with your friends?

_____

_____

How good are you at being obedient to your parents? (Score yourself 1–10.)

_____

What chores come naturally to you? What chores do you need to learn to do better or work harder at?

_____

_____

4. Now consider your spiritual strengths:

What is your prayer routine? Do you pray when you wake up? When you go to bed?

_____

_____

What is your favorite mystery of the Rosary?

_____

What is your favorite story from the Bible?

_____

Is there anything you have a hard time talking to God about?

_____

_____

When was your last confession? Are there things you want to get off your chest and ask God to heal? Are you in need of God's mercy and forgiveness?

_____

_____

Do you remind yourself about the Real Presence of Jesus when you receive Holy Communion?

_____

5. Now consider your emotional strengths or weaknesses:

What makes you happy?

_____

_____

What makes you sad?

_____

_____

What makes you angry?

_____

_____

What makes you irritated?

_____

_____

What makes you nervous?

_____

_____

What other strong feelings do you have?

_____

_____

How are you doing so far managing your feelings?

_____

_____

How do you express your happy feelings of excitement, success, or anticipation?

_____

_____

What is your typical reaction to your negative feelings?

_____

_____

Can you be peaceful and calm when necessary? Or are you often anxious?

_____

_____

6. What are you giving back to God now, and what do you plan to give back to God in the future?

_____

_____

Chapter Reflections

While discussing this chapter, my Dad gave me some extra advice about . . .

_____

_____

_____

While reading this chapter, I learned these two important things:

1. _____

2. _____

I resolve to live out the *LoveEd* teachings from this chapter by . . .

_____

_____

_____

Finish this chapter with the following prayer:
Lord, Jesus, thank You for creating me. Thank You for loving me. Thank You for teaching me how to love You. Thank You for my parents. Thank You for giving me people to love in my life. Thank You for showing us the way to live. Amen.

My Dad and I completed this chapter on

_____

(date and time)

CHAPTER 4

What's Going On Inside?

> " I praise you, because I am wonderfully made; wonderful are your works! "
>
> Psalm 139:14

There was quite a lot that Joey had yet to learn.

"Let's put it this way," his dad told him. "You just learned who you are: You are a unique person, with intellect and free will and all the Joey talents God so badly wanted the world to have. You also learned where you are: in the friendship circle with Rob and others and in the family circle with all of us here.

"Now you need to learn where you're going next. You can expect big changes in your body in the next few years because you're on your way to becoming a man. After that, you'll learn what you need to get to the romantic circle–how your heart and soul need to change along with your body. And then–"

Mr. Sullivan stopped talking. He seemed to be caught up by another thought. Joey wasn't sure what was going on.

"And then what, Dad?"

"Then it will be up to you what kind of man you decide to be. Because what we're talking about here, Joey, is a superpower. It's the power to create life, with God. You will have this power, Joey. And with great power comes great responsibility.

"God created all things. He spoke the world into existence and placed the sun, moon, and stars in the sky. Everything that exists was created by God, the ultimate Author of Life, and all that He has made is good. That is the truth of the nature of God's creation. It is through this creation that we are led closer to God and is almighty power and love.

"God created Adam, the first man, out of mere dust. Adam was given dominion over the earth, including the fish of the sea, the birds of the sky, and the animals of the land. Although none of these creatures were like Adam, God asked him to care for them. This first man was made in the image of God and blessed with a soul that would live for all of eternity. All human beings since Adam have been given this same gift.

"In the first book of the Bible, the Book of Genesis, we

read that God said, 'It is not good for the man to be alone. I will make a helper suited to him' (Gn 2:18). God went on to create all the wild animals and birds and fish, but none of these proved to be the helper Adam wanted. So out of Adam's rib, God created Eve. She was a beautifully different person, the first woman and specially designed to be the opposite sex. God created two kinds of human beings, then: male and female. Both kinds are made in His image, and together, man and woman reflect God's creative love. Man and woman were made by God to be a gift to one another.

"Then God said, 'That is why a man leaves his father and mother and clings to his wife, and the two of them become one body. The man and his wife were both naked, yet they felt no shame" (Gn 2:24-25). God also commanded them to be fertile and multiply, to fill the earth and subdue it.

"God, in His perfect wisdom and generous love, placed within Adam and Eve's bodies the power to create new human life. This is a privilege to cooperate with God in cocreating new life with Him. God created Adam and Eve to love one another and to care for their family.

"This is one of the most important ways that our parents reflect the creative love of God to the world.

"From the very beginning of creation, God wrote the body language of marriage within the male and female bodies. God intended that a man and a woman would share life together in this holy union and, through the love they share, bring new human life into the world to glorify Him. Married love is meant to be like God's love, which is faithful, fruitful, and unconditional. When Eve gave birth to her first child, she was amazed and said, 'I have produced a male child with the help of the LORD' (Gn 4:1). From that moment on, each person has come into the world as a tiny baby, cocreated by God and two parents: one mother and one father.

"Is all this making sense so far, Joey?"

Even though it was a lot to take in, Joey nodded and waited for his dad to go on.

"That's good, son. So each person is born as either a male or a female baby. The male baby grows to become a boy who eventually develops into a man, and the female baby grows to become a girl who later in life matures into a woman. The image and dignity of God is given to both wonderfully created sexes, male and female.

"Now, many, many, many generations later, where do *you* fit in?

"God created your body to work in fascinating ways. Imagine how all the systems of your body are working inside you so you can see, hear, digest your food, eliminate waste, circulate your blood, and breathe. The human body is truly amazing!

"Many of these things take place, not because you choose for them to happen, but because God set them in motion when He first created man and woman.

"God designed each person with many automatic control centers called glands. There is one gland in the brain that sends signals through our bloodstream to tell our body to grow. This gland is called the pituitary gland. When we're children, the pituitary gland sends growth hormones into our bloodstream that tell our bones, muscles, and other tissues to grow. A child's growth may depend on the rate his or her parents grew and on the size his or her parents grew to be. Some people will be short, and others will be tall. Stocky, thin, or wide—people come in all shapes and sizes. But each person is unique and special to God.

"Your body also changes shape as you grow. When

you're five years old, you're not just a taller baby. You stand differently, and you have longer bones and less of a belly. Your head is in a different proportion to your torso and legs as well. The same is true for adulthood. You're not just a 'bigger child.' Your body undergoes physical changes as it matures into a man.

"Your body is first made for the family circle; you start out helpless, needing to be cared for, and unable to speak or walk. As your body changes, you're able to enter the friendship circle; you can walk with others, talk to others, use your hands to help, and open your heart to share. You still have one circle left to get ready for, however: the circle of romantic love. This is the circle you enter where you pre-pare for your own family circle later."

Next, Joey's dad told him about how he can prepare for the circle of romantic love.

Getting Ready for the Circle of Romantic Love

"From the beginning of life, all the body systems, except one, are fully working. The one that isn't working yet is the reproductive system; that one doesn't start developing until we're in our preteens or teens. There is a particular time of our growth called puberty when a boy grows into a man and a girl grows into a woman. Puberty is the beginning of what we call adolescence.

"During adolescence, while our body is growing, our soul must also grow in love and grace so that we will better reflect the image of God in our

hearts, minds, and wills. It's up to us to work with the help of God's grace to grow in virtue and love so that we will be spiritually, mentally, and socially mature when we become fully physically mature.

"The time of puberty usually lasts about four years. Puberty usually occurs between the ages of eleven and seventeen for boys, with the average age being fourteen years old. For girls, the average age to reach puberty is thirteen, but anytime between the ages of nine and sixteen is considered normal. Puberty is a time for the body to grow bigger, not just in height and weight, but also to mature into adulthood so that a person is prepared to possibly be a parent when he or she is married. So, at puberty, the pituitary gland sends out another type of hormone known as a maturing hormone.

"What happens at puberty? A girl's body begins to change into a woman's body, and a boy's body begins to change into a man's body. During puberty and adolescence, a person's thoughts and emotions change as well. It might seem confusing at first, but the new changes will become more balanced as you grow over the next few years. Just as it takes time to learn how to talk and how to walk, it takes time to grow into a woman or a man. It also takes time to understand how marvelously God has created the human body, and why He has designed us the way He has.

"God created puberty so one day you could bring new human life into the world when you're married. It's amazing that God has so perfectly designed our bodies that we can actually cocreate life with Him! Having children is part of God's great plan for marriage. God made us out of love in order to love and be loved. We're to reflect His creative love to the world as husband and wife within the Sacrament of Marriage."

The Truth About Love and Marriage

Joey's dad went on. "You'll start to develop new feelings as you go through puberty. What are these new feeling for?

"Your own life began when your mother and father entered the circle of romantic love, met, got married, and started a new family circle—the one with you in it.

"Only God can create an immortal soul, but He chooses to create each human being with the cooperation of their earthly mother and father. In the holy Sacrament of Marriage, the hus-  band and wife provide the opportunity for God to bring a new human life into existence through their loving embrace. It's God's plan that each child come into the world born out of the love between a husband and wife within the Sacrament of Marriage.

"In the Sacrament of Marriage, a man and a woman give themselves fully, freely, faithfully, and fruitfully to each other. The wedding is such a great occasion in their life that they celebrate this in church, in front of God, asking for His blessing. They invite all their friends and family, asking for their support and prayers as well. In their marriage vows, the man and woman promise their faithfulness: 'to be true in good times and in bad, for better or for worse, in sickness and in health' and 'to love and honor' one another all the days of their lives. When they give themselves to each other in this sacrament, they give their whole person, body and soul, and offer their lives to God.

What's Changing . . . and What to Do about It

"Like I said, you'll soon be entering into a very important stage in your life," said Joey's father. "It's when you will change from a boy into a man. We'll talk about how you need to change in your heart and soul . . . but let's focus on your body's changes for now and how to handle them.

"Let's start with **your chemical makeup**. Puberty starts in the brain. Your pituitary gland releases chemicals that tell your body to grow. Your body then creates hormones that make your body change shape and size. In boys, the main hormone is testosterone; in girls, it's estrogen. In the next few years, your voice will become lower and deeper. That is triggered by your glands. So is your sweat and body odor. You'll have to shower more often, start using deodorant, and pick the right place to put your stinky shoes!

"Next, let's talk about your **changing appearance**. During puberty, you're getting stronger on the outside. Your bones will thicken. Your shoulders will broaden, and your rib cage will widen. Women get curvier during puberty; boys get a little more 'thick.' Your facial structure will be remodeled as well. You will also grow hair in new places. Not everyone ends up having to shave his face right away during puberty, but you will grow hair under your arms and around your genitals. And you may notice your Adam's apple growing while your voice changes. All these changes require more food to fuel them. You may have started to notice the change in your appetite already. Boys your age start getting hungrier. One slice of pizza used to be enough. Now, it takes three or four to feel full. That's why your big brother gets larger portions at the table than you do.

"Okay, now let's move on to your **sexual organs**. The new physical changes during puberty include another important thing: the growth of your reproductive organs—penis, testicles, and scrotum. The penis is the male sex organ that provides for the release of urine and semen to the outside of the body. The testicles are two ball-shaped organs in a male that produce hormones and the reproductive cells called sperm cells. The scrotum is the soft pouch of skin on the outside of the body between a man's legs that contain the two testes (testicles). The testes are the main organs that release the large amounts of the male hormone, testosterone, into your blood stream that causes all these changes in you at puberty.

"During puberty, a young man will probably experience erections more often. This is a hardening of the penis due to an increase of blood flow in that area. An erection can happen due to stress, excitement, or boredom; it can occur during sleep, upon waking, or for no reason at all. It's normal for erections to happen to boys at puberty, but erections can also happen to boys of any age. If ignored, the erection will go away on its own. It's wrong for a boy to rub or stimulate himself to cause or prolong an erection. If a young man does nothing to cause the erection, there is no sin. Similarly, if a young man is tempted to entertain impure thoughts or actions but resists those thoughts, there is no sin either. A young man can train his mind to say a quick prayer and to think of other things that are good and wholesome. If erections are experienced often due to boredom or stress, try some good ways to release built up energy or tension. These would include daily exercise, more active sports games, and keeping busy and active doing good deeds for other people. The good old-fashioned cold shower can also help.

"Another normal thing that happens is that the male's body releases excess sperm cells through a process called a nocturnal emission, more commonly called a wet dream. At times he might wake up at night with an erection or wake up confused and find that liquid semen containing the sperm has been released from his penis. This occurs naturally and is no cause for worry. It may just be time to learn how to change your bedsheets! Wet dreams occur less often as boys move through puberty, and they eventually stop.

"We should also talk about your **spiritual growth**. Sometimes these emotional changes spill over into your spiritual life. When we're children, we might have a good relationship with Jesus Christ and feel we can always talk to Him and be His friend. As these increased male hormones impact our life, we might become moody in our faith life, too. But truly, this is a great time to go deeper in your faith. You will start to have deeper questions. Don't hesitate to find the right people and ask them. We will talk in a later chapter about how to handle this.

"Last, let's talk about your **emotional changes**. You'll experience different emotions—sometimes you might be grumpier than normal; other times, you will be happier than ever. These mood swings are normal; they're due to chemicals inside you. You just need to plan for them. Some boys make the mistake of embracing the new anger that they feel: They start listening to angry music, watching angry movies, and playing angry video games. Others learn how to better handle their moods without being unpleasant toward others.

"Let's talk a little about managing your anger," said Mr.

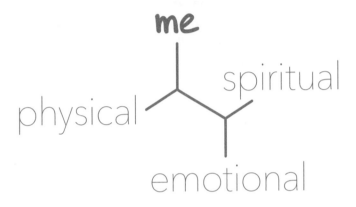

Sullivan. "I'll start with a story."

Joey was fine with that. He liked stories.

"When I turned eleven years old, I started feeling angry more often. I would sometimes get angry at my sister, sometimes I would get angry at my dog, and sometimes I would explode when my mother asked me to do things. I even got mad at the TV once and broke the remote—and the wall. But that's another story.

"I wasn't always sure why this happened, and I always felt bad afterward. It seemed like I spent every day apologizing for doing something wrong, and I started to feel bad about myself.

"One day my mom—your grandmother—said, 'Maybe your Uncle Joe can help you with your anger.' I didn't understand. My Uncle Joe was one of the kindest people I knew. Uncle Joe never seemed to get angry.

"So I asked my mom, 'How can Uncle Joe help me?'

"'Your Uncle Joe once had a terrible time managing his own anger,' she said. 'Let's call him up and see if he can meet with you this Saturday.'

"Uncle Joe and I spent Saturday together. We stopped at the park and threw the baseball back and forth while he taught me how to think before I act. Uncle Joe helped me learn little ways to practice self-control over my actions no matter how I was feeling inside.

"Like me, you may feel strong emotions, Joey," said his dad.

Joey was alarmed. "But you hardly ever get mad!"

"Sure I do. I just keep it under control," Mr. Sullivan answered. "And you can, too. Just like Uncle Joe—who you were named after, along with St. Joseph."

Learn How to Manage Your Emotions

Joey's dad had more to say on how to manage emotions.

"Emotions can be managed without hurting others or ourselves. Good physical health, good exercise, good friends, a good prayer life, and the support of our family can help us learn to experience our good and bad emotions well. Here are a few ways you can learn to manage your emotions positively.

"When you pray, you're training your mind to focus on God instead of your problems. You're learning to turn to God for everything you need. When you choose to help others instead of being selfish, you become more mature and more cheerful, too. The emotional changes you experience are all part of a good process—a process designed by God to help you mature. You may wonder what this has to do with puberty or purity. If you learn to manage your feelings now as a preteen, you'll be able to manage more challenging feelings when you get older.

"Talk with us more, Joey. We are your parents, after all. Sometimes boys and girls feel ashamed about their thoughts and feelings during puberty. They may feel that they are the only ones who have ever thought such thoughts or felt such emotions. You may feel like we still treat you like a little child. Remember that we were once preteens, too! We want to know what you're thinking and feeling. Spend more time with us; that way, we can better understand the growing 'new you.'

"Turn to us for guidance. We've already been through puberty and adolescence. Consider us to be your 'coaches' for virtue. Think of a sports coach that's teaching and encouraging you to score and win. We want you to win at life! Humbly accept our guidance, try to talk things out with us instead of arguing, and ask us for suggestions on how to be a better person. Unfortunately, some preteens pay more attention to their sports coaches than they do their parents. Remember that this game of life requires obedience to your parents in order to win the eternal prize.

"Puberty is not a time to give in to temptation and rebel, even though you're growing in independence. Instead, discuss your need for independence with us and listen to our concerns as well. Talk and listen, and we'll all grow in understanding of one another.

"It's important for young men to remember that young women are also going through physical and emotional changes and to be extra kind to women if their moods seem to change from day to day. Women's monthly cycles include a series of hormone changes that sometimes are difficult to understand. While men have a much simpler hormonal cycle, women are more complicated physically and emotionally. A good man will understand this. These differences between males and females are the beginning of the challenge to understand the opposite sex as we grow into adulthood and approach a possible marriage in the future."

Be Not Afraid

"Listen, Joey. St. John Paul II's favorite saying from Jesus was 'Be not afraid.' This is a great motto for young people entering puberty. There are big changes ahead, but Jesus Christ is with us, and He is bigger. With Him by our side, we can say, 'bring it on.'

"Puberty is not going to mess up your life. It will make you stronger. So be not afraid!

"Try to understand that you'll feel more balanced as you grow over the next few years, and learn to manage your behavior rather than live according to your whims and feelings. Just as it took you time to learn how to talk and how to walk when you were a baby, it will take some time to grow from a boy to a man. The discomfort and confusion you might experience during puberty are only temporary while your body is making hormonal changes. Be patient with yourself, and pray. It takes time and wisdom to understand how marvelously God has created the human body, and why He has designed us the way He has.

"Your friends will likely all be at different places with what they know about puberty, love and marriage, and the transmission of life. Discuss with your parents how you should manage where and with whom you talk about these things.

And remember, if you experience anything that concerns you, or have a bodily change that you didn't expect or don't understand, that is the time to talk frankly with me or your mother or another caring adult who knows you well. God has put your parents in your life to guide you through every change and each challenge as you grow up.

"Puberty is not simply 'happening' to you. Puberty is the time in your life when you learn how to take charge of your body, your emotions, and your spirit. Taking charge of all aspects of yourself is a lifelong process, but it starts now. As you develop healthy, holy habits during puberty, you will be participating in God's special plan for you. He wants you to grow up to be a holy and mature man!"

Discussion Questions

Talk about each item on the list below with your Dad. Which ones are you doing already? Mark the following practices with one or more of these three signs:

✝ Practices you already do well

? Practices you want to understand better

T Practices you want to "try"

Physical

- ☐ Eat the right foods.
- ☐ Get enough sleep.
- ☐ Keep your body safe.
- ☐ Keep your body clean.
- ☐ Avoid indecent images; they can stick in your mind.
- ☐ Exercise—it increases the "happy hormone" in your brain.
- ☐ Do some hard work, like helping your Dad clean out the garage or planting a garden with your mother.

Emotional

- ☐ Develop self-control over your words and actions.
- ☐ Practice thinking first before acting on a feeling or emotion.
- ☐ Experience your emotions in a healthy way that does not harm yourself or others.
- ☐ Avoid the useless drama that accompanies puberty; help friends stay grounded.
- ☐ Express yourself through music, dancing, writing, or art.

☐ Find a new way to express yourself, such as painting, skateboarding, or chess.

Personal

☐ Learn new things and develop your talents.

☐ Develop hobbies and interests.

☐ Work hard in school so you can be the best you can be (this is a time when you will develop mental skills you use the rest of your life).

☐ Find out where your most constructive passion is, and spend a lot of time on that (building, organizing, exploring, dissecting, reading, growing plants, caring for animals, studying, etc.).

☐ Find ways to help others, such as washing your neighbor's car, or mowing the lawn, or babysitting for friends at church.

Social

☐ Learn how to be a good friend to others.

☐ Find friends who support you on your journey to heaven.

☐ Learn how and where you can contribute positively to our society.

☐ You will have a strong tendency to fit in, so avoid situations that will change you for the worse.

☐ Talk about your feelings with your parents.

☐ Give yourself to others in need.

☐ Learn how to get along with different types of people.

Spiritual

- ☐ Pray to God, and ask Him to shed light on what you are to do with your emotions.
- ☐ Ask God to carry your burdens.
- ☐ Sing some songs of praise to God and enjoy being with Him.
- ☐ Spend some time out in nature, and thank God for creating our world.
- ☐ Go to Catholic youth events and practice keeping your mind open to what the speakers share.
- ☐ Read books about defending the Faith; develop a passion for the truths of our Faith.
- ☐ Don't leave tough questions unasked; find someone who can answer them.

Chapter Reflections

While discussing this chapter, my Dad gave me some extra advice about . . .

_____

_____

_____

While reading this chapter, I learned these two important things:

1. _____

2. _____

I resolve to live out the *LoveEd* teachings from this chapter by . . .

_____

_____

_____

Finish this chapter with the following prayer:

God, our Father, thank You for creating me in such a marvelous way.

I thank You for life and health. Keep me in awe and reverence for the sacredness of my body.

Help me always to respect myself and others. Amen.

My Dad and I completed this chapter on

_____

(date and time)

CHAPTER 5

The Battle for Purity

> Do you not know that the runners in the stadium all run in the race, but only one wins the prize? Run so as to win. Every athlete exercises discipline in every way. They do it to win a perishable crown, but we an imperishable one.
>
> I Corinthians 9:24–25

Joey's dad took a deep breath.

"Listen, son, I know this is a lot of information to take in over our past few weeks of talking. But these things are important for your growth as a man. We can continue to review it whenever you want. Always let me know if you have any questions or if you hear something we need to discuss. I want you to know the truth about God, the truth about yourself, and the truth about what love really means.

"You're at the beginning of a new and exciting journey

as you grow from a boy into a man. This time of puberty and adolescence is a dividing point in your life. You're the one who decides what kind of man you're going to become. It's time for you to journey forward, to continue to discover the world and your mission to share God's love. God created you for love, and as you walk the path of love, God wants you to *learn* to love and to *choose* to love.

"Getting to the destination would be easy if the path was smooth and clear, but the path of life is often rough and difficult. Remember the story of Col. Roger Donlon? The reason he was so well prepared for battle is that he had developed so many virtues during his childhood and adolescence. The world we live in today is carrying on a battle against the family and against purity. That's why all those virtues we have been talking about are important for you in order for you to become a loving person.

"As you journey through life, the battles you face may not be in the military; they could be right inside of your heart and mind, inside your friendships, and inside all the choices you make. This is an important journey—a time to discover your talents, choose new friends, get a good education, develop important virtues, and learn how to act when romance comes into your life. You need to think ahead and prepare. You have to know where each path leads, where the dangers are, and how to make it safely to your destination.

Strong, Smart, and Pure

"Remember the three important words that will help guide you in the years ahead: strong, smart, and pure. Let's take a closer look at each of them.

"You might ask, **'What does it mean to be strong?'** Yes,

it means being physically strong. But we need strong souls as well. A strong body can run, lift, and push. A strong soul can run from temptation, lift people up, and push through great sacrifices. Your soul needs to 'hit the gym' as well so you can strengthen your will to become a great human being. And here's what a spiritual workout looks like: Each time you resist the easy choice and choose the challenge, or resist selfishness and choose the good of another, or just plain resist wrong and choose right, you grow in spiritual strength.

"Being strong also means being in control of your will. Take control of what you think, what you say, and how you act. Did you ever see a ninja ready to fight his enemies? He's in control. He has a strong will to make the right moves. Think about what's right before you act. But when you happen to mess up, be a strong person and have the courage to apologize and try to fix what you did wrong.

"Next, you might ask, **'What does it mean to be smart?'** Being smart is more than passing a test in school or knowing how to build a tree house. First of all, being smart means knowing who you are, where you came from, and where you're going. Being smart is knowing what love is. Real love is sacrificing yourself for the good of others. Real love is caring for other people, not just for yourself. Real love is your mom and dad working hard to give you a good education. Real love is being patient with your

little brother or sister and not always getting your own way. Love means being kind to your friends, respectful toward girls, and obedient to God. Learning how to love your family and friends now will help you practice for your future as a loving adult.

"Smart also means knowing who's been on this journey before you: people like us, your dad and mom, and maybe your older brother or uncles. They can give you guidance on your path and answers to life's questions. Think of how much Uncle Joe helped me learn to deal with my anger. It wasn't always easy for me to control my anger, but each day as I made one good choice after another to control my reactions, it slowly became a part of me until all my family saw was my virtue.

"And you should get to know the lives of other heroic men. Men like St. Joseph, who protected Jesus and Mary; St. Francis, who resisted the evils of his time to care for the poor; and St. John Paul II, who loved hiking up mountains and acting in plays and who had the courage to tell people the truth about God, even when his life was in danger.

"To grow stronger, you'll need the virtues of truthfulness to fight off lying, generosity to fight off greed, forgiveness to fight off anger. You'll need self-control and confidence in God to fight off alcohol and drugs, and responsibility to fight off vandalism. And in your entertainment choices and in real romance, you'll need chastity to fight off lust. All these virtues will help you keep your relationships pure.

"And lastly, **'What does it mean to be pure?'** The dictionary says purity is something that is clean, clear, unspoiled, and free from contamination. Something pure is original; it has no additives or artificial ingredients.

"Athletes avoid junk food and instead eat a healthy diet of pure, whole foods. We call having a healthy body filled with nutritious food physical purity. But what about the purity of your soul? Lots of the stuff you see and hear on TV and the Internet are like junk food for your soul. These things can fill you up with the wrong ideas about love and friendship, about how to act with girls, and what it means to really love someone. You'll have to be really strong and smart to keep that kind of junk out of your mind. And you'll need regular confession to keep junk out of your soul.

"Purity is also like a window. The cleaner the window, the more you can see on the other side. Having a pure mind and heart will let you see clearly the goodness and beauty of other people and also see what God wants for your life. The purer you keep your window, the more spectacular things God will show you through it.

"Sexual purity always keeps in mind God's purpose and meaning regarding human sexuality. We know God has placed a higher meaning in us when He created us.

"Since we express the love of God through our bodies, what does purity look like for a man who lives purity? Real men are protectors, and you need to protect yourself and your friends from impure things.

"Here are some practical ways you can live a pure life.

"In the world today, a young man needs to do all that he can to avoid the occasions of sin against purity. The ninth commandment states, 'You shall not covet your neighbor's wife.' This includes coveting any woman, even if she is not married. Jesus said, 'Everyone who looks at a woman with lust has already committed adultery with her in his heart' (Mt 5:28).

"Lust is using people or looking at them as objects of pleasure. Lust destroys love. Lust is the opposite of sexual self-control; it's acting on your feelings rather than acting according to God's plan for love. Christ's warnings about lust are an invitation to a pure way of looking at others, a way of controlling our thoughts, and a way to respect women by seeing them as friends and treasured daughters of God.

"Let me ask you a question, Joey. When you see a girl who's immodestly dressed, should you stare?"

Joey thought for a moment before answering, "No. I don't think so."

"That's right, you look away. Why? Because real men respect women and treat them as people, not objects. In your relationships with girls, chastity will help you focus on your friendship with them instead of romance. Learn to love them for who they are, not because of the feelings they give you. It will take some practice, when those new hormones begin to flow, to see the inner beauty of a woman and not to be distracted by her body parts. It's definitely easier to see a woman's dignity when she dresses with dignity. However, not all young women dress modestly these days.

"Unfortunately, immodesty and indecency are all around us. It may be that you need to look away, say a prayer, or think of your favorite sports or other interests when faced with a difficult situation. When watching TV, try to become quicker with the remote control in order to change channels when commercials or shows become impure or indecent. And you may have seen billboards on the highway that have beautiful women on them that advertise an 'adults only' bookstore, or clubs for 'mature men.' Mature men would not go into one of those stores or clubs. Those places are designed to stir up lust and have nothing to do with love.

"Indecent pictures, books, movies, and websites are called pornography. People today make a lot of money trying to stir up lustful desires in others. Looking at indecency can even harm your ability to love your future wife. When you see it, and you know it is indecent, look away and ask God to remove it from your memory.

"Here's a purity challenge: To begin, you'll need to work on 'custody of the eyes.' Custody of the eyes, or 'purity of vision' as the *Catechism* calls it, is the practice of turning your eyes away from the sight of a woman who is immodestly dressed. Why do men need to do this? Because the sight, sound, or smell of a beautiful woman can take over a man's imagination and easily lead to lustful thoughts or the idea that she is an object for pleasure. A man with a pure mind and heart trains himself to see the beauty of a young woman who is made in the likeness and image of God—a person who deserves respect.

"To stay pure, you will also need to learn to use good judgment in your choice of entertainment. The media gives you polluted messages that makes sin look like normal, acceptable behavior. The characters in the shows are looking for love in places where God is missing. A chaste man does not toy with evil or lie to himself saying, 'I'll just watch this indecent show once,' or 'The words of that song do not affect me,' or 'I'm only curious.' Listen, Joey, a pure man will avoid music and entertainment that might fill his mind with the wrong messages about sexuality. Music and movies that present lust as normal can have a slow, brainwashing effect on you until you begin to believe that sexual sin is normal behavior. Real passionate love belongs in marriage.

"Next, be very careful on the Internet. Use Internet controls to filter out the bad stuff. If someone sends you an indecent picture or note on your phone or computer, delete it immediately and tell that person to stop. Block their number if they continue. That way you're protecting yourself and you're helping to protect them as well. Make good friends with other kids who are trying to be pure. This will help you avoid temptations and make better choices.

"Remember the story Pope Francis told young people about the Devil and his team? Today there are more and more ways the Devil tries to con you into joining his team instead of Jesus Christ's team. Just because there are more ways to join doesn't make it any more right. Your duty now more than ever is to stand with Jesus and refuse to budge."

Practicing Chastity

"Now," Joey's dad continued, "let's talk about protecting your chastity. Chastity is the virtue that directs our sexuality and sexual desires toward authentic love and away from using others for sexual pleasure. The virtue of chastity will help you to keep your thoughts and experiences of romantic love pure and according to God's plan for you. Chastity helps us control our sexual desires and places them at the service of God's love in marriage.

"Many good achievements in life require practice. Think of the effort it takes to become a great musician, athlete, or student. Think about how many daily baseball practices a player needs to attend when he is on the all-star team.

"When practicing chastity, we love people without thinking sexual thoughts about them. We first love the people in our family. We can work on building a closer relationship with our parents. We can spend more time helping them and doing what pleases them. Developing good personal relationships with your brothers, sisters, cousins, and friends helps you learn how to love, too. These are great opportunities to practice unselfish love, which is a great preparation for family life later on.

"When you're older and mature enough to date, practicing chastity means respecting the purity of the girls you spend time with. Never touch them in an immodest way— respect the fact that they will be wives one day. Even later on, when you're engaged to the woman you hope to marry, practicing chastity includes avoiding those particular hugs and kisses that are only appropriate for married couples. A chaste man leads himself 'not into temptation' by avoiding those situations that can put his purity at risk. Did that sound familiar? It should, because those words come from the most famous prayer in the world, the Lord's Prayer.

"Being chaste means respecting the truth and meaning of God's plan for marriage in thought, word, and deed. Don't tell jokes about people's bodies, especially their private parts. Don't talk about sex in a casual way or use foul language. Don't talk about sexual topics with your friends.

Instead, turn to us, your parents, for correct information. Remember that God made your body and He lives in you, so use clean language, choose pure entertainment, and pick friends who do, too.

"As you practice chastity and keeping your thoughts close to God's, you will learn how to see a woman's beauty as something holy, something to be revered. A beautiful woman does not have to be a temptation to sin but should be an opportunity to appreciate the beauty of God. Only people with a pure heart are truly happy, because they're able to love God and their neighbor."

Mr. Sullivan knew this was the time to remind Joey about the real source of strength for practicing chastity.

"Now, Joey, do you understand why we have to become strong at all those other virtues before we become a man and have sexual desires? It's so that we're up to the challenge when we face decisions in purity and chastity.

"The only way to grow really strong in virtue is to turn to God for His help and grace.

"Your spiritual training for the virtue of chastity includes:

- spending time in personal prayer in order to develop a deep and personal love for God,
- studying the *Catechism of the Catholic Church* in order to be strengthened by the truth,
- reading and meditating on Holy Scriptures to learn about and love Jesus Christ more,
- receiving the Eucharist and the Sacrament of Reconciliation frequently—spiritual food for the journey,
- offering personal sacrifices to God regularly,
- and serving others for Christ's sake and expecting nothing in return.

"To practice chastity, begin to resist any impure thoughts that come to your mind and ask God to help you have pure intentions as you appreciate the friendship and beauty of women.

"If you should feel urges and desires of attraction for women, know that these attractions are good and thank God for them. To avoid lustful thoughts or actions, you can do three things: First, call upon God for His help. Second, remind yourself that those feelings are supposed to be reserved for marriage. Offer your thoughts and actions to God for your purity, your vocation, and the purity and goodness of all marriages in the world. Third, act—go find something *good* to do!

Heroes for Purity

"Look at the heroes we cheer on in the movies. Whether it's Spider-Man, Batman, or Luke Skywalker, so many movies feature a hero who would lay down his life for the dignity of a woman. He wants to rescue others with his heroic actions. He wants to fight evil and do good. Men enjoy these types of adventure stories so much that they're called 'guy flicks.' These movies have guys running to the box office, lining up for tickets, and coming back for the sequels! Men want to be heroes—in their minds and in their actions. They want to win battles, and they want to be admired for what they've done.

"St. Paul knew this about guys when he was speaking to the men of Corinth. He said:

Do you not know that the runners in the stadium all run in the race, but only one wins the prize? Run so as to win. Every athlete exercises discipline in every way. They do it to win a perishable crown, but we an imperishable one. Thus I do not run aimlessly; I do not fight as if I were shadowboxing. No, I drive my body and train it, for fear that, after having preached to others, I myself should be disqualified. (1 Cor 9:24-27)

"The most important decision we Catholic Christian men can make is choosing to run the race to heaven with Jesus Christ, who is the Way, the Truth, and the Life. Like the olympic runner who strives for the gold medal against fierce competition, a Christian man runs the race and wins the treasured trophy by his dogged diligence. With God's grace and the support of his family and friends, he tries to get through times of temptation and discouragement.

"God has promised that our prize will be greater than the gold, silver, and bronze medals of the olympic athlete. It will be the prize of eternal life. Although that prize may seem far away for now, God offers earthly rewards as well; a better life in union with Him when we see that His 'will be done, on earth as in heaven' (Mt 6:10).

"What sacrifices are you willing to make to glorify God with your mind, will, and body? Would you do hard work for it? Would you train yourself untiringly? Would you sacrifice having your own way? Would you practice self-mastery and keep your mind and actions pure? Would you do anything to protect the purity of the girls that you see and meet? Would you do everything you can to prepare yourself for your future vocation? Would you stand up against the enemy and fight for the goodness of God?

Role Models for Purity

"St. Joseph, the husband of Mary and foster father of Jesus, was a pure and chaste man who remained a virgin his whole life, even while married to Mary. He was chosen by God to be the protector of Mary and Jesus, and he loved them both very much. When God spoke to St. Joseph, he listened and followed  His directions. As a husband and father, St. Joseph was kind and respectful to Mary and took the time to teach Jesus his carpentry trade. St. Joseph is the patron saint of chaste men. It is a good idea to pray to St. Joseph each day for the virtue of chastity.

"Another great example of purity is St. Maria Goretti. She preferred to die rather than allow a man to commit a sexual sin. The family's farmworker, Alessandro, tried to force himself onto Maria to get her to commit an impure act with him. Maria refused him so he would be spared that sin, and Alessandro stabbed her to death. Maria was so holy that she forgave her murderer as she died."

Joey interrupted Mr. Sullivan. "Dad, remember I'm only eleven years old! I have time to prepare for this battle and this race and this journey. How should I start?"

"Good question, son. Keep up the good work you're doing to grow in virtue and learn more about who you are as a person."

"But how do I do that, Dad? What does it mean to know myself? I'm just Joey, right? The guy who's always picking up Legos and taking out the garbage and playing with the little kids. That's who I am!"

Mr. Sullivan smiled. "Yes, Joey, that's true, but as you grow up, you'll ask yourself questions about the meaning of life, and God has all those answers waiting for you. You're a special person made in the image of God! And you were made to love. You can become a better friend and better family member by getting to know yourself in light of God's love and developing your talents and gifts in order to serve Him better.

"This is the time to discover your personal strengths and weaknesses, your talents and desires. Will you be you more of a thinker, a watcher, a talker, or a doer? What are you good at? Are you talented at music, sports, cleaning, running, reading, or building? How do you get along with others? Are you bossy, shy, impatient, too loud?

"You can learn more about your personality and talents by working with others. How do you participate in a group science project? Are you the one who takes the lead, follows others, or sits back and lets the others do your work for you? If you're in clubs, notice how you react to others and what contributions you make. When at home, do you obey promptly and get your chores done first? Do you wake yourself up in the morning so your parents don't have to? Ask yourself, 'How do I get along with my brothers and sisters?' Do you act so kindly to them that they love to be around you?

"Maybe you're funny or brave. Think about how you can use your talents to make other people happy. If you're funny, you can make people laugh when they're sad. If you're brave, you'd have the guts to convince your friends to choose the right thing. If you're trustworthy, then people can tell you things they're afraid to tell others. Know yourself. Try to see yourself as God sees you and how others see you. This knowledge can help you if you use it to improve yourself so you can respond with maturity to the upcoming challenges of independence and adulthood.

Help for the Battle

"There's one more important thing to learn on this journey, Joey. God loves you and wants to be with you every step of the way. God wants you to be strong. He has given you a free will so you can make good choices, especially about love and purity. He has given you the Sacraments of Communion and Reconciliation to strengthen your soul. God wants you to be smart. He's given you an intellect so you can understand His plan for life. And He gives you His wisdom through the Church, the Bible, your parents, and your teachers. Finally, God wants you to be pure. He gives you a desire for true love and beauty. So as you travel the road ahead, make a courageous effort to become strong, smart, and pure. These trusty guides won't ever let you down.

"To grow in strength, pray to St. Michael the Archangel, who called on the power of God to defeat Lucifer, the rebellious angel. You can call upon God's power by asking for St. Michael's help in battling against temptations to sin. The Devil wants you to misuse your sexuality, but God's grace is stronger. Fill your mind with good and pure thoughts, stories of saints, adventures, and great achievements. Perfect virtue may not happen all at once, but with practice, you can grow stronger and control your thoughts and imagination.

"Great challenges require heroic responses. If you stay close to God and His will for you, you will have courage to be one of the heroes of this generation. Be a hero for purity!

"You were created out of love in order to love and be loved by God. You can make God's pure love visible in the world through the choices you make to live a life of goodness and virtue.

Stand up for the truth with your life. Love God with a passion. Be a champion! Your perseverance in virtue can change the future of your life and the lives of many others. If God is calling you to the priesthood, your life of holy celibacy can speak to the whole world of our ultimate destiny of union with God.

"You can have a part in changing the future of the family. Take the challenge and use your God-given powers wisely. Live the truth, fight the battle, and never give up. An eternal reward awaits you at the end of the race!

"If we want to do battle against the Devil, we need powerful allies. Like I said, St. Michael is the angel who led the battle in heaven against the Devil. We want him on our side. So say the famous prayer to St. Michael as much as you can: *St. Michael the Archangel, defend us in battle. Be our protection against the wickedness and snares of the Devil. May God rebuke him, we humbly pray. And do thou, oh Prince of the heavenly host, by the power of God, cast into hell Satan and all the evil spirits who prowl about the world seeking the ruin of souls. Amen.*"

Discussion Questions

Answer and discuss these questions with your Dad.

1. Who in a Bible story or another book or movie plays for the Devil's team? Who plays for Christ's team?

_____

_____

_____

2. Have you ever done something bad and felt terrible afterward? Did you ever do something good but difficult and feel great afterward? How does that show the different strategies of the Devil and Jesus?

_____

_____

_____

3. Where are you most likely to see indecent or immodest images in your community, home, or school? How can you avoid those situations?

_____

_____

_____

Chapter Reflections

While discussing this chapter, my Dad gave me some extra advice about . . .

_____

_____

_____

While reading this chapter, I learned these two important things:

1. _____

2. _____

I resolve to live out the _LoveEd_ teachings from this chapter by . . .

_____

_____

_____

Finish this chapter with the following prayer:

Jesus, I want to be strong, smart, and pure like you and all the saints. Thank You for the Church to guide me and my family and teachers to lead me on the path to real love. I want to love You and love others in a pure way here on earth and stay on the journey toward eternal love with You. Amen.

My Dad and I completed this chapter on

_____

(date and time)

CHAPTER 6

Joe's Big Adventure

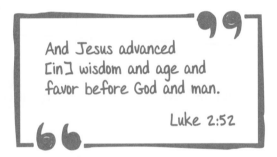

> And Jesus advanced [in] wisdom and age and favor before God and man.
>
> Luke 2:52

Joey found himself staring out his window again after his dad left, only now the view had changed.

He didn't just see what was in front of him; now, he saw the great circle of God that was all around it.

God had created enormous planets hurtling through space way off in the distance above the sky, and God had created the big bright sun to light all of it up. But God had also created Joseph Andrew Sullivan, and He had given Joe (he was feeling more "Joe" than "Joey" all of a sudden) something He didn't give to the planets or the sun.

He could know things, and he could decide things. And suddenly he wanted to know more and more and get better and better at making the right decisions.

One day—and that day was coming closer all the time—Joe Sullivan would be a man. He needed to start preparing now.

Far above him, in heaven—a place he could only imagine—things were very busy. Prayers were pouring in from all over the world. Mothers prayed for their children in war-torn nations. Men in prison prayed for a new direction and a second chance in life. Families in financial crisis prayed for what they needed. God, in His providence, took it all in.

Then another prayer came: *"Dear Lord,"* prayed St. Joseph, *"please send Your Holy Spirit to inspire Joseph Andrew Sullivan."*

God, in His infinite wisdom, heard all of these prayers and looked after all of these people. But He also paid attention to Joe. Ever a wise manager, He knew that one strong Christian man would have an enormous effect on the world. A boy who deliberately formed himself to be a force for good would affect his family circle and his friend circle, and all the people in both those circles would affect the people in *their* circles.

God knew that Joseph Andrew Sullivan deciding to be a great man would not just change Joseph Andrew Sullivan, and it would not just change his family. His good actions and positive choices would have a ripple effect that would help the people around him in ever widening circles.

If Joe were loyal to Rob, then Rob would grow in confidence and be nicer to his sister, and if she in turn helped out a friend, and if that friend helped her family, and if the father of that family decided to do things a little better at work, and if someone at work was inspired to help his or her own family, it would go on and on—the consequences of Joseph Andrew Sullivan doing good, in God's hands, would spread far and wide.

God knew that the kingdom of heaven grows like a mustard seed, that small beginnings grow into huge trees. God also knew that the kingdom of heaven was like yeast, that a tiny amount raises the dough of the whole world.

So God answered St. Joseph's prayer for his special namesake, Joseph Andrew Sullivan.

A question occurred in Joe's mind: What kind of man do you want to be? Now is the time to decide.

Joe decided he didn't just want to be a man. He wanted to be a man of God who was capable of being a hero. He wanted to be a man capable, with God's grace, of making great sacrifices for others. He wanted to be a man capable of building big things with God. He wanted to be a man who played hard for Jesus's team, a man who didn't fall for the lies of the Devil.

"What's gotten into you, Joey?" asked Michael.

Joe hadn't noticed that his brother had come into the room.

"Call me Joe," he said. Michael was about to ask why, but something about Joe's smile made him stop.

"Okay, Joe. Listen, Greg is going to give me three tickets to Kidz Funzone. I asked mom and dad if you can go, and they said sure. I don't know who should get the other ticket though."

"A strong, smart, and pure man needs to be loyal and thoughtful," Joe thought.

"Can we give it to Rob?" he asked.

Michael frowned. "Greg doesn't like Rob, does he?"

Joe answered, "He doesn't even know him. I'll talk to Greg about it."

"Okay," said Michael. "I'll text Rob. The tickets are for this Sunday afternoon."

Joe went downstairs. Ava had made a big mess getting her own lunch. Joe cleaned it up, and in the process, noticed that the trash had filled up again with cereal boxes, an egg container, and a milk carton. He took it out without being asked.

"You have to be responsible for small things before you can be responsible for great things," Joe thought.

He saw that the mail had come, so he brought it in. It was a big bundle today, with catalogues, a newspaper, and a newsletter. The mail carrier had put a rubber band around it. He took the rubber band off and dropped it down on the table. Immediately, one of the catalogues dropped down and flipped open. It was a clothing company selling women's swimsuits.

First he had this thought: *"Hey, you are going to be a man soon. You will be entering the circle of romantic love. You need to know what girls are all about. And these girls are very pretty."*

He had to admit, all this talk about puberty had peaked his curiosity. Thinking about changing bodies made him want to see girls' changing bodies, a little.

Then he had this thought: *"Are you kidding? I don't need to look at pictures to know what girls are all about. And I shouldn't use anyone as an object just to be looked at."*

He had to admit that was true, too. He had just learned that it's a really bad idea to look at pictures like these.

But another, stronger thought came: *"Girls look nice. There is nothing wrong with looking at girls. You are built to enjoy their beauty. What's the harm?"*

Joe froze for a second.

"Lord Jesus," St. Joseph repeated, high in the heavens, *"please send the Holy Spirit to inspire Joseph Andrew Sullivan."*

Then one last thought came to Joe: *"When temptation comes, don't play with it. Run!"*

Joe headed out the side door of the kitchen, dropping the catalogue in the trash on his way out.

"The devil is trying to trick me," he thought. *"I play for Jesus's team, and each one of those girls was created by Him for something great. He died for them. I should be willing to die for them, too."*

Joe's day didn't change all that much from the day before. But in another way, everything was different.

He was no longer Joey, a boy with small role in a small family in a small house in a big world. Now he was Joe, a boy who was growing into a man, a man who had the opportunity to work directly in Jesus's plan for the world.

He was also a boy who had a trip to Kidz Funzone in his near future.

Joe did a lot of things different that week, just like he had planned:

He talked to his parents more. Not a lot more but a little. He had to think of things to talk to them about at first. He asked his mom why she married his dad. But then more things naturally came up—he asked them questions about high school and what they thought he was good at.

He talked to Greg about Rob. The next time Greg and Michael were hanging out, Joe told Greg about the time Rob and he met a bear in the woods. Rob knew what to do, speaking in a clear voice and then walking slowly away at a diagonal angle. When the bear followed them, Rob had them stop, and then he spoke loudly and waved his arms. The bear got scared and ran away. Joe could tell Greg was impressed.

Joe kept control of his emotions, too. On Saturday morning, after working extra hard on his chores, his dad wouldn't let him go over to Rob's house but just kept giving him extra chores. At first, he got mad—especially when Michael was allowed to leave to work cutting lawns even though he had only done half of his chores.

A thought came to him: *"You're working so hard on being a man, and they treat you like a little kid."*

But then another thought came: *"I want to be the kind of man who does the right thing whether people notice it or not."*

On Sunday at Mass, Joe had a hard time concentrating, even though he was an altar boy and really should've been concentrating. He was thinking about going to Kidz Funzone that afternoon. Besides, Father Ed's homily wasn't about adventure this time. His homily was about the importance of keeping your faith even when you go on vacation. There was not a lot there for Joe to think about.

It was after Mass that Joe faced the hardest part of his new "adventure."

After extinguishing the candles and putting his robe away, Joe finally came outside to see Greg walking away with his family and Michael looking slightly stricken.

"Bad news," he said. "It turns out Greg was wrong. He thought he had three tickets to Kidz Funzone to give us, but he only had two. You're going to have to tell Rob he can't go."

It was not as though images flashed through Joe's head, but certain thoughts did in a way. Joe thought about George Washington at Valley Forge, and then he thought of Roger Donlon dragging the sergeant to safety as he got wounded in the face. He then had a strange image of St. Michael wearing a JC jersey and diving to stop a ball from going into a goal.

Then he thought of the future Joseph Andrew Sullivan, now a man.

"If you're okay with it, would it be all right for me to send Rob with you instead of me?" he asked.

Somewhere, St. Joseph smiled.

Closing Prayer & Meditation

Now comes the most important part of the lesson: bringing all of this to God. Here is a meditation you can do in a church—or in the quiet of your room.

Place yourself before God. You don't make Him present; He is present already, all around you. Simply become aware of Him.

God is as real as the air you breathe and the electricity keeping your light on, even though you can't see Him.

And He loves you. He loves you so much that He created everything you have ever enjoyed in life and everything you will enjoy.

Tell Him: "Lord, I adore You. Your greatness is infinite. Compared to You I am a speck of dust, and yet You still care for me! You are all-powerful, all-knowing, almighty—and all-loving."

Thank Him for filling your life with so many good things: the people who love you, the food you eat, the clothing you wear, the home you sleep in.

Tell Him you are sorry for any sins you have committed. Maybe you have even committed sins against purity. That is nothing to worry about. Jesus is stronger! Tell Him to give you the strength to fight against temptation and sin, and ask Him for the grace of always confessing sins in the Sacrament of Reconciliation as soon as possible so you can keep up the fight!

Then, thank God for the gift of your human soul and body.

Thank Him for the gift of freedom, which allows you to choose your own path in life. Without freedom, you couldn't love, you could only follow a single path of instinct or natural forces. Tell Him: "Thank You for this great gift of freedom.

I want to give the gift back to You by choosing You in all things."

Thank Him for the gift of your reason. Without your mind and your ability to learn, you would not be able to wonder about things; you would not be able to experience the joy of discovery, the joy of seeking—and finding—the truth. Tell Him: "Thank You for my reason. I want to give this gift back to You by using it to seek out Your will and the glories of Your creation."

Then thank Him for your body. You have the ability to do astounding things physically. You can build things; you can go places; you can swim, climb, and throw a ball. Now that your body is maturing, you will have even more power and more responsibility.

Fish glorify God by swimming; that is God's plan for them. Giraffes glorify God by eating leaves on the savannah; that is God's plan for them. Human beings glorify God by choosing to fulfill the plan He has given us, to live out His virtues in the family circle, friendship circle, or romantic circle.

Tell Jesus that you want to use your body according to your will and your reason to do what glorifies God in your life.

Tell Him you are willing to do whatever He asks of you. Perhaps that will mean the priesthood. It will usually mean married life. But whatever it means, tell Him you are at His disposal.

If you do this meditation in a church, look at the tabernacle. If you are not at a church, think of Jesus in the Blessed Sacrament.

Thank Him for coming to us in His Body, Blood, Soul and Divinity. Thank Him for His Real Presence. Then think of Him there, choosing to look like a host of bread. A host has no arms. A host has no legs. A host has no mouth. He chose to look like that so that we would understand what He wants from us.

When we receive Him in Communion, everything changes—then He has arms, and legs, and a mouth, because He has ours.

Tell Him: "Jesus, you need a body in my community, and I need Your love in my heart. Let me give You my body to use to do Your will in the world, and You give me Your love in my heart so I can have the strength to do it."

The future can be scary, mostly because it is unknown. A lot of changes come with puberty. But the future is exciting, too—a whole new adventure. Thank Jesus for bringing you to this point in your life, and invite Him to walk by your side through to adulthood.

Mary is ready to help you, too. She is your mother, and she is praying for you already. Pray a Hail Mary to her, and slowly pray an Our Father and Glory Be. Then offer your day to Jesus.

Notes